Naked Sunfish: *Best Bites*

Rick Brown

All texts written by Rick Brown and previously published in *Naked Sunfish*.

www.nakedsunfish.com

ISBN 978-0-557-72842-8

Printed in the U.S.A.

Forward

In this irresistible collection of short stories, plays & ramblings ... lifted from the virtual pages of NakedSunFish.com ... Rick Brown draws his readers into his world, filled with human chia pets, air guitar playing dentists, and an assortment of characters shared from his own life experiences.

I have known Rick for well over ½ my life ... and he has always been a writer. In the early years, there were songs ("Silver Lady", "Round and Round", "Song for a Friend", "Cowboys are Assholes") and his ubiquitous journals ... large black bound volumes always nearby ... filled with what I assumed was the happenings to and around him.

Then, in the early years of the internet, his friend Ted Kane asked Rick contribute to his web-zine, *CrapShoot!*. Rick's writing began to shift in purpose and style ... no longer written for just his own pleasure ... but for a broader audience.

Since 2002, Rick has edited and written for his own web-zine, Naked Sunfish. In the almost 9 years that have transpired since Issue #1, Rick has found his voice ... a voice that is reflected in the stories here ... filled with insight, wit and humor.

So regardless if you nibble on these stories from time to time, or devour them in big bites, be prepared to be drawn into Rick's unique world.

Enjoy...

Dan Eley ~ 2010
Webmaster
www.nakedsunfish.com

Introduction

Welcome to Naked Sunfish.

If you're wondering about the name...and I'm sure you are...I'll try to come up with a clever explanation. Just don't count on one. Naked Sunfish was originally an idea for a musical/art group a buddy of mine and I planned to form way back in high school. Initially it was to be a sort of Christian psychedelic pop/rock/folk band...a myriad of contradictions if you will. The celebration of opposite polarities. Intensive diversity that so blurred the lines...so elevated the gray areas...that the audience would forget we were constantly trying to contradict ourselves and see only a new vision floating like a cloud above the fracas. (Kind of like Las Vegas) Unfortunately...through circumstances TOTALLY under our control...our intellectual experiment de-evolved into a goofy solitary gig as "Harry Legs and the Little Shavers". Fun for us. Confusing for others. (Which...in some bent way could be argued a successful fruition of the premise) We spent WAY too much time playing 8-ball in my friend's basement rather than practicing. (Yet another argument for philosophical success?)

There ARE ulterior motives. Perhaps some one surfing the web using the term "naked" might just come upon the SUNFISH. And if you know anything about sailing you will remember that a Sunfish is a very, very tiny sailboat. My wife and I ventured out on one many years ago off the Jamaican coast and ... because of my highly polished skills ... almost took us to Cuba. We were not naked when the wind caught the sail but could easily have been upon our arrival. I felt as if we were being swept away by Hurricane Whoever. The wind in my hair. the sight of a rapidly shrinking Jamaica.

Once I realized my significant other was frantically screaming, "LET GO FOOL! LET GO!!"...and I did...we slowed to a comforting drift. It took us 10 minutes to travel what seemed half way to Havana and almost an hour to zigzag back to Jamaica. That's as close to buying Cuban cigars legally as I've gotten. And I haven't tried to sail a tiny boat since.

So...in the spirit of NAKED SUNFISH...both the adolescent philosophical stab at intellectual/deconstructive/existentialist mayhem AND the terrifying exhilaration of possibly screaming across the Atlantic in a tiny sailboat quite possibly beaching NAKED on the shores of the Land Of Fidel...with some help from my friends...is yet another web site (like we all need one huh?) There will be music. There will be politics. There will be art. There will be food and drink. There will be nonsense. There will be most definitely sarcasm. There will be NO rules. NO deadlines. NO consistency. NO traditions. ("The illusion of permanence," as Woody Allen so aptly put it) Enjoy the ride whilst you can. Because some day ... sooner or later...I'll be sure to hear some one screaming at the top of their lungs, "LET GO FOOL! LET GO!!!" And I probably will.

Rick Brown
January 23, 2002

"I may still be a fool but I haven't let go yet."
Autumn, 2010

Everything here is random. Nothing is in chronological order...not how things went down nor when written down. Yet everything is for the most part true...enhanced perhaps but never fictionalized. Because if there is one thing I have learned in this life it's that the shit that happens is...more often than not...weirder than any shit I could make up. I celebrate the mundane mostly because unlike those who wallow in it clueless...I think it's hilarious...albeit tragically at times. And when they are not annoying the living crap out of me...I find those very wallowers entertaining as well.

53 Horsepower

For some reason us Baby Boomers had a love affair with the Volkswagen Beetle. I'm unclear as to why when I look back honestly. I've owned several of these cult cars, known as "Hitler's Revenge" to my father and anyone who fought in World War II. My wife Yvonne learned to drive in a Beetle. And up until a couple years ago never drove an automobile with an automatic transmission. VW has marketed a "new" Beetle and had great success selling it...although everyone I've known who has owned one doesn't have much good to say about the vehicle. I drove one for a few days while my Miata was having some body work done and believe me...I was quite elated to have my faux British sports cars back.

So why was the original car such a hit? It was cheap. I bought my first Beetle...as in Super...brand new in 1973. At first I loved the thing. (The Thing was actually a different VW model...but that's an entirely different tale.) It wasn't long before the nagging little things that go wrong with Beetles regularly began happening. The passenger's side window crank had a habit of breaking off in the rider's hand while cranking down the window. And although these little beasts went great through the snow...and always seemed to start on cold days...the heater...or lack thereof...was a big...BIG problem. Even when the heaters worked...which was in about 20 percent of the cars produced...they were problematic. Take my 1973 Super Beetle for example. It had a great heater...too good as a matter of fact. I jokingly referred to the settings as "being of only two distinct levels". HELL! And "off".

But the heat was the least of my worries. About 18 months into ownership I was driving with Yvonne one fine day when the accelerator cable broke. Since the engine was in the rear of the car a cable ran from the gas pedal back through a small channel...out the firewall where it connected directly to the throttle of the carburetor. Now some of you might be impressed by all this automotive jargon I'm throwing out here. Don't give it a second thought because none of these parts actually exist anymore. Anyway...the cable had a fragile little "s" hook that merely slipped into a hole underneath the gas pedal. High tech huh? And that stupid thing was constantly braking off. So on this, the very first time it happened, Yvonne and I were taken by complete surprise and left up to our own invention as to a remedy. Fortunately I had a pair of vice grips in the car. While Yvonne tried to lay on the floor with the vice grips clamped tightly on the broken cable, I instructed her as to how far out she should pull the cable while I attempted to shift through the gears. This hot summer afternoon still stands as one of our finest moments as a couple. I learned soon enough it was much easier to carry a replacement cable at all times than to rely on vice grips. This discovery also gave me the freedom to drive all by myself.

As I said earlier, I've had several Beetles...some good...many not so good. (I distinctly recall a yellow one that I once ended up kicking the shit out of in a busy intersection...quite a scene. I lovingly nicknamed it "Lemon".) But the very favorite Volkswagen I ever owned had to be the 1964 Microbus. It was the old style with the split front windshield and opposing side doors that open out in opposite directions. AND...it had been converted into a camper! Not one of your stock dealership campers, mind you...but a funky cross between acid trip/fishing lodge décor. Inside was that cheap paneling you used to be able to buy at places with names like "Paneltown" (There actually is a Paneltown here in Columbus. As a matter of fact that's where we bought flooring when we remodeled our kitchen last year. We got a great deal...from the

Mayor of Paneltown.) But the coup des grace was that it had been painted LIME GREEN!!!!

And just in case you are desperately wondering...yes the accelerator cable on this hippie van broke constantly also. In fact, one time after my buddy Dan and I had run the Cleveland Marathon...in the rain...we were forced to crawl under this behemoth and fix...you guessed it...the accelerator cable! In the rain. After running 26.2 miles...in the rain. Those were the days! You can see how Volkswagen had this strange spell over people's memories.

Anyway, despite the idiosyncrasies...despite all the work of adjusting the valves...changing the oil every 3500 miles...changing cables...the popping out of third gear on occasion...the ultimate slowness of the vehicle (It's air cooled rear engine logged in at a powerful 53 horsepower.)...I had tons of fun in this mobile party pad. One St. Patrick's Day it was dubbed, "The Mean Green St. Patty's Day Machine". It took groups to the Lake Erie Islands...camping in the Hocking Hills. Lot's of people had great adventures in this old lime green hippie van. But the biggest adventure of them all was surely the vacation Yvonne and I took to Cape Ann, which is a beach area just north of Boston.

This was by far the longest trip ever taken in the

1964 Microbus. The two of us had it loaded to the gills for a week in the sun, on the beautiful Massachusetts' shoreline. Little did we know, getting there would be the story. I mentioned briefly earlier that this albatross had a mere 53 horses pushing behind it. I hadn't thought much about this until we got to the mountains in the western section of Massachusetts. It wasn't so much that these were...by any means...huge ass snow covered mountains. By Ohio standards sure...they were big. But I've been to Germany and there are much larger ranges there. And that's where they assembled our vacation wagon. Soon I discovered that if there was anyway we were to actually make it to the top of a mountain, I had to get this green monster moving as fast as possible DOWNHILL just for the CHANCE to make it up the next incline. That meant a 1964 VW Microbus/Camper (in lime green) doing no less that 92 miles per hour! You haven't yet lived...or come close to a horrible death...if you have never been traveling downhill at 92 MPH in a vehicle whose front wheels sit directly under your ass!! The first thing that entered my mind...besides the "why is this thing shaking so damned much"...was the reality that in between my legs and (hey pick any moving object...a dump truck full of slag shall we say)...in between my legs and a dump truck full of slag was a sheet of metal about 3/8 of an inch thick. At 92 mile per hour...downhill...in a 64 VW bus...this is not an uplifting epiphany. Thoughts of going through the rest of my days with nothing below my knees rushed into my throbbing brain. The only advantage to losing one's legs below the knees that I could come up with were that then...and only then...would you be able to ride comfortably in the backseat of a VW Beetle. I was truly uncomforted by this thought.

But if screaming downhill in the Massachusetts' mountains was anything but terrifying then trying to make it uphill was equally embarrassing. By about a third...just a THIRD...of the way back up the incline the lime green hippie machine immediately began slowing down. And by the time I had the thing halfway up the mountain...and I am NOT exaggerating here...I had the bus in second gear doing perhaps...oh...18 miles per hour! TOPS! And the noise! AYEE! An air cooled 53 horsepower reared mounted motor straining to push it's cargo up a mountain is deafening...a deafening BAAAAAAAAAAAHHHHHHHH!!!! Yvonne tried to speak to me. I mean...I saw her mouth moving but all I heard was BAAAAAAHHHH!!!

"What?" I yelled. Still...more mouthing and just BAAAAAAAHHHHH!! Then right before the crest of the incline...on say the fourth mountain...about half a mile from the top...one of the most embarrassing things to ever happen to me occurred. I looked into the big side mirror and saw...much to my amazement...a tractor trailer with a "Wide Load" sign lashed on the front...a tractor trailer pulling a modular home...not a trailer...a fucking MODULAR HOUSE!...turn his blinker on and move into the fast lane to pass. I was beside myself. I began to swear up a storm. "JEEEEZZZ UZZZ FUQUE ING KEEE RIST!!! I was yelling so loud Yvonne even heard me over the constant BAAAAAHHHH!!

By the time he came up alongside us we were doing maybe 12 miles per hour. BAAAAAAAAAAAHHHHHHHHHH!!! I turned away as he crawled past. I couldn't look the other driver in the eye. Who could? BAAAAAHH! Glancing into the rear view mirror I saw what looked like the parking lot on a busy day at Disney World. There must have been 150 cars impatiently waiting to go past a 12 MPH hippie van and an 18 MPH tractor trailer pulling a modular home with a "Wide Load " sign strapped to the back! And of course over the hill I had to go as fast as possible downhill for the next mountain...as did the guys pulling the "Wide Load" It dawned on me just then to let him by. Otherwise there would be a repeat of the world's slowest drag race each time there was a mountain ahead. And on every frikkin' hill it was second gear....BAAAAAAAAHHHHHHH!!!! But soon Mr. Wide Load was ahead...out of sight. And I'll tell ya...it's a lot less embarrassing doing 18 MPH while the engine is deafening you with BAAAAAHHHHH!! when the vehicles passing you are going 65. They zip by you without looking.

We got to our destination safely. I believe the drive out and back must have cut off 3 days from our beach time. Yet we made the best of it and had a great vacation. Actually, sleeping in the lime green hippie van was more fun than driving it on the freeway. We made it home in one piece too...still have our legs below the knee. But if anyone tries to tell you what great cars the Volkswagen Beetles and Microbuses were...well...think of me driving up that mountain...BAAAAAAHHHH!...at a walker's pace. Perhaps my father had a point. Maybe it was Hitler's Revenge.

When to Buy a New Lawnmower

When I was a boy my father...to earn some extra cash...had a little lawnmower repair shop out back in the garage. So I know a bit about the machines...and thought he did too. Actually he did. But after I gave up on the push mower...the purist's type with no engine at all...he gave me his. My wife and I had just purchased our house and since the yard was far from flat, pushing a 49 year old reel mower got to be quite a chore. Now I had my very first rotary mower. And although it seems dumb to me now I was pretty excited.

It was some generic brand from someplace like the Andersons a generic mower from a generic store. I didn't care. It was fire engine red with a 2.5 horsepower Briggs and Stratton and a bag on the back. A shiny...relatively new...rear baggin' lawnmower. This kind of stuff can get a guy going...at least when it's your first. Sure it was a cheap $99 store brand...but it was Homeowner Rick's first foray into power tools. BRRUMM!!

The first summer or two it was fine...although the novelty DID wear off when I realized it weighed like...oh...7 tons. This was way back in the days before safety features that shut off the motor when you're not mowing or stopped the blade if you weren't pushing it. In other words...like older lawnmowers before it...it was DANGEROUS! By the third summer the red paint wasn't so shiny. It didn't run so well. I probably didn't take as good care with it as I should. I may (or may not) have hit it with the car in the garage. Depends who you ask. But I figure if a man can't abuse his lawnmower what CAN he abuse? Possibly his weed whacker...I've used those as a javelin...but that's another story altogether.

The real big problem started when the lever that held the bag on the back started failing. Lawnmowers vibrate a lot and sometimes by the end of the chore the clasp would have loosened up considerably. Eventually that very latch holding the rear bag all the grass clippings were jettisoned into got real...real...sloppy. I had to keep an eye on it and tighten the damned thing up every 10 minutes or so. Otherwise I assumed...all hell would break loose. Little did I know how prophetic my concern turned out to be..

One excruciatingly hot...humid...August afternoon...the kind only people living in the Midwest...or directly on the Equator can know of...I decided I better get off my duff and mow the friggin' grass. The charm of cutting the grass had long since turned to dreaded drudgery...even under the coolest conditions. And I had already waited too long. In

August...if you have a lawn like mine...when it hasn't rained for a while...the weeds in the lawn get to be say...18 inches tall. So even though your grass...or however much there is of it...is turning brown and dormant...you're not so much "mowing the grass" as "evening up the weeds". So I needed to make the 4-inch high grass and the 18 inch weeds even with each other at about 2 1/2 inches. The lawn hadn't turned brown yet. It was right at the cusp of dormancy...still green and in need of mowing. I knew if the job didn't get done this day soon my yard would look like the set of "Gunfight at the O.K. Corral" complete with tumblin' tumbleweeds.

Because it was at least 900 degrees with 300% humidity I shunned modesty...put on a pair of shorts, shoes and a headband. I figured at least this way my misery might lead to a little suntan. I started the mower...only took 37 yanks on the cord. Already I was sweating profusely. I mowed behind the garage. Sweat poured off me like a waterfall. I mowed the side and front yards. I felt my shoes getting soaked with sweat. Now all I needed to do was the dreaded backyard with it's picnic table moving...doggie doo doo dodging...don't accidentally hit the flowers...exhilaration. My pulse quickened at the thought that in 20 minutes I could be home free. But the totality of the brutally hot afternoon's karma was teetering on disaster. I had...in my haste...disregarded the lever holding the bag on the back of the mower.

What happened next was like a backyard simulation of the Big Bang Theory. As soon as the bag was almost completely full of grass, dust, and weeds...that faulty little lever holding the bag to the back of the rear baggin' rotary mower...gave up the ghost. Immediately the bag BLEW off the back and in one giant FFFFWWWOOOOPPP! what seemed like a BAIL OF HAY smashed into my sweat ridden body and face. I was literally covered head to toe in grass clippings, weeds, dust, and quite possibly doggie doo doo. To say I was outraged is understatement X 1000. I began to swear in languages I didn't know how to speak. "You mutha fukkin' goddamned son of a fukkin' lousy cheap ass". I was alternating kicking and spitting on the still running...still belching debris lawnmower from hell. I was possessed with anger and like a GIANT GODZILLA CHIA PET I stomped and kicked and swore and spit and kicked and stomped and swore and spit...in an effort to destroy Tokyo...er...I mean my mower.

Finally...after it dawned on me that I could hurt myself...BADLY...I turned the damned thing off. Still sweating and covered with half my backyard I heard some mumbling in the new silence of the aftermath. I turned to my right and...in the street that runs alongside the house...I saw 6 or 7 little children...none of whom could have been over the age of eight. They all had a look of terrified wonder on their cherubic faces. It was as if they had just witnessed something awesomely surreal. It was a look like "We should tell Mom and Dad...but they won't believe a giant six foot Godzilla Chia Pet assaulted a lawn mower." I do believe the event forever changed the way they looked at life...perhaps not in a good way. It was then I realized...people were trying to raise children in this neighborhood. And they didn't deserve to see something like this on a hot summer day in their carefree youth. I decided then and there...YUP! It's time to go out and buy that brand new lawnmower I'd been thinking about since April. You see...I HAD to do this...for the sake of the little children.

Coming of Age

    I suppose there are a few perks to being the oldest of four. But for the most part...and I've surveyed others who are the first born and have siblings close in age...as the oldest, your mom and dad are honing their parenting skills on *you!* I had to live up to a higher standard most times than my younger brothers and sister. And the fact that my mother had all four of us in fewer than six years just amplified this reality for me. It certainly seemed to me that *I* had to be the best *behaved* (We'd expect that of Jimmy and Donny...but you?) and that *I* had to be the most *patient* (You'll have to wait until you're 12 before you can ride your bike on the street.). I got used to the behaving thing (I made up for it later in high school!) but the *waiting.* As the oldest I'd wait...try my best to be patient...and as soon as I was allowed to *do* something...well...that's when the parental units CAVED!! All of a sudden all *four* of us could do it...even though I waited the longest. But hey...it's not like I carry this around with me. It's not like *I'M STILL REALLY, REALLY PISSED OFF ABOUT IT OR SOMETHING!!!!!!*

Ahem.

Like I said earlier...there were a couple perks being the oldest. The best was when I was say 9 or 10 years of age. I got to stay up a little bit later than my brothers and sister could. And since my mother got up at 5 a.m. (or so it seemed) she went to bed many times before I did. So that left me with my dad...just the two of us in our own tiny black and white T.V. watching world. Now if there were two things in this life my father adored, it was watching television...and eating. He was fairly indiscriminate about both really. Yet this private time with my father has grown to be perhaps my fondest memory of him...those two years or so that it existed. It felt special then as it does to this day.

Our favorite T.V. show to watch together was The Red Skelton Show. Freddie the Freeloader, George Appleby, Gertrude and Heathcliff...it was all good. And while we were a poor, working class family it seemed to me that nothing tasted better while watching Red with my dad than say...saltine crackers with peanut butter and jelly on them. Or a fried bologna sandwich. But the best of the best was SARDINES!!! My father first introduced me to the canned delights packed in oil...on white bread...Wonder bread or Millbrook... either brand was the soft, pliant gooey white bread with no air holes. (Like air holes taste bad right?)

My father ritualized sardine sandwich nights. I would follow him out to the kitchen where he pulled the key off the bottom of the sardine can...cranked the can open...and drizzled out the excess oil. Then he would pull each little fish out...cut the tail off...slice it down its belly...and remove what he called "the guts". He meticulously carved each sardine this way while I stood at his side watching. This became a ritual...*our ritual*. And except for the nights when the key broke and it took almost running the car over the can to get to the sardines...I loved our ritual.

Later, my father introduced me to sardines packed in *mustard.* YELLOW mustard!! A lot of people...even back in the late 50's...turned their noses up at sardines...especially those floating in yellow MUSTARD!!! Consuming sardines packed in mustard was like thumbing our noses at those uppity folks. At least my dad made me feel that way...that somehow we were rebels watching television and eating sardine sandwiches. To hell with those who put down T.V.!!! In your face anti-sardine snobs!!! HA! HA! These are the ones packed in MUSTARD!!! While he never verbalized this...it's what I took away from the experience.

One evening...close to the end of our special time alone...right before my brothers were invited to join the T.V. snack club...we went to the kitchen together for the sardine sandwich ritual...during a commercial break in Red Skelton of course.

"Ahhh!! Here are some packed in MUSTARD!!" I remember him joyously proclaiming. And as always he carefully pulled the key from the bottom of the can...wound open the top revealing the little treasures lying in yellow mustard. He cut off the tail of the first fish and placed it on a slice of white bread with no air holes. He took a second fish...cut off the tail and laid it on the bread next to the first. And after he broke tradition for the third time I was confused.

"Dad?"

"Yeah?"

"Aren't you going to take out *the guts*?" I reverently inquired.

My father looked down at me...grinned...and said earnestly, "Ricky...I think you're big enough now to...*eat the guts*!!"

Forget the fact that he was probably getting sick of

cutting tiny fish down the middle and removing *"the guts"*. Maybe it got to be a chore for him. There are times when the reality of something is beside the point.

All I know is that at the age of maybe 10 years old...upon hearing my father announce that I was now big enough to eat sardine guts...I stood there...looking up at him thinking, "Wow...I'm BIG enough to eat *the guts*!! With my dad...just us two."

We carried our plates into the living room where Mr. Skelton was waiting for us. My dad and I devoured our sardine sandwiches...on gooey white bread...with YELLOW MUSTARD...with *"the guts"*.

And I felt proud.

The Non – Fiction Theater of the Truly Mundane
proudly presents:

Eye Poke

Scene: an eye doctor's office circa 1960. The waiting room is an industrial green in color with a drab gray counter. A receptionist sits behind the counter. Steel framed chairs with black vinyl cushions line the walls. Smatterings of people sit randomly around the room reading old magazines. A 9-year-old Ricky is seated fidgeting, next to his father, who is affectionately known to Ricky's cousins as "Snook". Ricky is obviously rambunctious.

Ricky (whispering just a little too loudly) – Daddy?

His father leans down towards his son.

Snook – yes?

Ricky (in the same inappropriate whisper) Sometimes my wiener sticks up!

His father seems visibly taken aback, somewhat embarrassed, at a loss for words.

Snook (in an authoritative tone also a bit too loud and inappropriate) – Well…just *LEAVE IT ALONE AND IT WILL BE OKAY!*

Curtain

Cast:

Receptionist – herself
Patients – themselves
Ricky – Ricky
Snook – Snook
Wiener- uh…you know.

Wacky Weed Whacker Wackiness

So I go home yesterday from what turned out to be a difficult day (another story) determined to get the yard trimmed before yet another rain comes. I paid the girl next door to mow last Friday so the lawn was okay...but it looked funny with 5 1/2 inches of grass sticking up around the wall, fence and patio. Out of all the homeowner tasks I dislike, this tops the list. Still, I knew I had to get it done or matters would just get worse.

Once in the house I donned my "weed whacking" outfit...a stylish ensemble of an old ripped up t-shirt, shorts (in much the same condition), the longest socks I could find without looking like a total dork (trimmers are much better at throwing rocks than whacking weeds), and, of course my Italian sunglasses ($5 at an open air market in Florence) which means they're really worth about 37 cents) to protect the one good eye I have. I gave my regards to Henri (my dog) and made my way to the garage.

Now I've had several of these weed trimmers. You know...the ones that have the plastic "fishing" line hanging out to clear out weeds or anything in its way. (I'll give you $1000 if you catch a fish with his stuff) I've come to the conclusion that there's not a good one on the entire market. No matter how much you pay for one...be it gas powered or electric...the majority of your time is spent cursing the thing while undoing the cap on the bottom so you can pull the line through again. Sometimes I have to do this 10, 11 times...and I won't even go into refilling it. I've had a love/hate relationship with every whacker I've owned. Mostly hate.

Sooo...I'm in the garage plugging together the 3 or 4 extension cords that it takes to get around the yard...although it also takes 3 or 4 "re-plugs" to get the job done...when I hear a car start revving up and speeding down Druid. We live on a corner and the side street (Druid) only goes for three blocks (thank God) so we don't get much traffic. And I really notice when some one is driving fast...and I'm in the garage which faces Druid. As the car races by me I drop what I'm doing, walk out to the street and yell, "Slow down FOOL!" (I thought about calling him an asshole but that word is used so often these days I believe it's lost its' impact. Actually, now I rely on words and phrases that are much more subtle...but since they aren't used so much guys don't know how to react to words like "fool". Ironically, it has more shock value...and Mr. T.

made a movie career AND pro wrestling gig out of saying, "I PITY the fool!" Think about it. I don't think people would have taken him seriously at all had he used, "I PITY the asshole!") So the guy hears me call him a fool and slams on the brakes at the stop sign...which is about 30 feet from where I'm standing. And what does he do? You guessed it. He gave me the finger...THE finger.

This sort of cracks me up. Giving somebody the finger is such a cliché anymore. I mean...in this rude, crude, MTV society of bad manners it doesn't mean...well...it doesn't mean ANYTHING anymore...at least not to me. I go to the CD shop and what do I see? A poster of Kid Rock giving me the finger next a poster of Eminem giving me the finger. Wow...how CREATIVE!! How REBELLIOUS!!! It bores me...really, really bores me. I mean...can't these "I'm pissed off for no apparent reason" artist (and I use the word loosely) types come up with anything more original? Jeez...how FIVE years ago! How Axl Rose-ish!! Giving me the finger...the cliché of the new millennium. Anyway...as he's giving me the finger I yell, "You drive like a MORON!!!" (This is another great, great word that isn't used much any more. Moron...I love it.) But I don't think HE liked it because I saw his backup lights come on.

OOOOH!! Now he's gonna get rough with me!!

So. I sauntered back into the garage and picked up my trusty weed whacker. (This is the original commercial name for trimmers I think...kind of like Kleenex is for tissues...and I have a REAL, ACTUAL WHACKER!!!) I must have looked pretty menacing in my dirty old t-shirt, long white athletic socks and cheap Italian sunglasses. Just about the time he reaches my driveway I come out of the garage...weed whacker in hand...finger on the trigger. I have this vein by my eye that sticks out when I'm "concerned" about something. You know...like Clint Eastwood...except his is on his forehead...and it's bulging!

"You WANT something?" I say as I pull on the trigger gingerly. VVVVRRRRRRRR, VVVVVRRRRRR, VVVVVVVVVRRRRRRR! I could see the "macho" just vanish from his face. VVVVVRRRRR, VVVVVVRRRR. I lifted the weed whacker up to car window level for effect.

"Um...why did you yell at me?" he asked sheepishly.

"There are KIDS in this neighborhood you know." I snarled at him.

VVVVVRRRRR, VVVVVRRRRRR, VVVVVVRRRR!!!!!

"But...but...I wasn't even driving that fast." he says quietly.

VVVVVRRRRRRR, VVVVVVVRRRRRRR!!!!

"Well it was TOO fast for MY street!" I say.

VVVVVVVRRRRRRRR, VVVVVVRRRRRR!!!! VVVVVRRRRR!!!!!

Know what? He just drove away...ever so slowly. Just high tailed it outta der pardner. MAN...this was as much fun as I've EVER had weed whacking! And I realize if they ever make a movie out of this they'll probably use a gas trimmer. It would provide more drama but the dialogue would certainly suffer...and of course the guy's car would crash and burst into flames after he drove off.

I'm thinkin', Nicholas Cage as homeowner Brown. Ciao baby.

Epilogue:

"Talk softly and carry a big stick." Teddy Roosevelt - 20th Century President

"Talk softly and carry a plugged in weed whacker." Rick Brown - 21st Century Homeowner

It Was Forty Years Ago Today...

Ah yes. The Summer of Love. 1967. *Sergeant Pepper's, Light My Fire, White Rabbit,* et al. I loved the music. Yet somehow I was totally ignorant of it being "The Summer of Love". At least until August of that fine summer. My parents helped me finance a spot on a Cleveland area charter bus headed to the American Lutheran Church National Luther League Convention in Dallas, Texas. Being a tender 15 years old at the time, it's an understatement to say I was excited.

Away from home for the first time...with my mom and dad's blessing! Wow. Now I really didn't know many of the other kids going. I attended school in a different town than most of the Luther Leaguers. So along with being ecstatic, I boarded the Greyhound with some anxiousness...trepidation. But soon enough we were joking, screaming, singing songs like "Salvation Army" at the top of our lungs. We were all on a terrific adventure together. This...is when I learned it was the "Summer of Love" from kids identifying themselves as "hippies". This was way cool...even for Luther League.

The bus stopped in Akron and picked up more Luther Leaguers. That's when I met Kenny. He was the first black guy I ever called my friend. Hell...he was like the 3rd black person I'd ever MET! Kenny was a couple years older than me. And he became my mentor of sorts. We wandered the streets of a city deep in the South where less than four years earlier John F. Kennedy was assassinated...where segregation still existed. Our youthful ignorance was incredibly blissful. I learned a lot from Kenny. He had...after all...lost his virginity. And he was proud of it.

I remember stopping by the old Ryman Auditorium (home of the Grand Ole Opry in Nashville for lunch. I was in awe. Outside of Lake Erie and a short jaunt into Canada I had never been *anywhere* in my short life. It seemed something new and exciting was happening every minute!

All the kids from my church stayed in a hotel called The Adolphus , an elegant old building that was overwhelming to me. I grew up in an old farmhouse. This Adolphus...it was a castle. And of course we all went crazy doing incredibly stupid things. Things like throwing a hamburger out a 15th story window to see if it would fly like a Frisbee. My favorite though was folding someone up in a rollaway bed…sticking them in the elevator…and sending them down to the lobby!!! We all wanted our turn. But the hotel manager eventually put the kibosh on that fun activity. And of course then came the obligatory lecture from our "sponsors" about behaving like young Christian Luther Leaguers. Bummer. Bummer in the Summer. Bummer in the Summer of Love.

I went to a dance one night early on in this long weekend of out of town exuberance…at a different hotel no less. And I did something extremely difficult for me at the time. I asked a girl to dance. In true "Ricky" form I chose to ask her during a song ridiculously impossible to dance to, The Young Rascal's cover of "Mustang Sally". But I managed to get through the tune doing my best "white kid having a mild seizure" dance style. Afterwards she told me her name was Beverly. I told her my name. Bev asked me how old I was. I didn't lie.

"I'm 15" I said. "How old are you?"

"17 but I'll be 18 soon."

I felt like I'd been sideswiped by a Mustang…talk about 19 – sixty six! Beverly wasn't a *girl*. She was a WOMAN!! And before I could put my flat feet back on the ground Beverly smiled at me. She didn't flinch. I fell in love. It was the summer for it. I walked her back to her hotel after the dance. I kissed her. I kissed a woman...well *almost* a woman. Close enough to make me feel like there was nirvana running through my veins.

Bev and I spent most of the rest of the convention together...not always AT the convention mind you. We danced...we walked in the Texas heat holding hands...sweaty hands. We watched Luther League sanctioned movies together. Then...on the final afternoon we decided to skip the convention altogether...some presentation on "healthy sexuality" and "responsibility" something along those lines. Emboldened by my new girlfriend (who was almost a woman)...with a confidence I had never felt before...I asked her if she would like to go to my room and...uh..."talk".

She said "yes".

Getting off the elevator I grew more and more anxious. What if my roommates decided to skip as well? Or worse...what if a sponsor caught us? Then...to add to my paranoia...down the hall from my hotel room...was a maid vacuuming!!! Oh my GOD!!! She could walk right in on us!! Call the hotel manager!!! Or the police! Beverly smiled. I put the "Do Not Disturb" sign on the doorknob hoping it would salve my worry. It did not.

The two of us chatted for a little while. Then we kissed. Then we FRENCH kissed. Then we made out with a passion new to me. My system was in overdrive. I said "Excuse me for a minute" and rushed to the door...flung it open...and yelled over the vacuum to the maid, "You aren't coming IN HERE ARE YOU??!!!!" The cleaning lady nodded "no". And I relaxed...for a while. Beverly and I continued our uh...discussion...and soon I found myself...my hand to be specific...touching her breast...outside her blouse. Beverly smiled. We kissed some more. Then I bolted to the door...again yanked it open and repeated to the confused...and amused...maid, "Are you SURE you aren't coming IN HERE?!!!" This time she laughed and yelled "I am NOT coming in THERE!!"

Why a pretty brunette woman/child from the middle of Iowa would continue to find me appealing at this point is still a mystery to me. I sat down next to her and we picked up where we left off. I decided to go to second base...a place I had never been. (Unless you count the couple times I actually got a hit in Little League...but I didn't count that.) I slowly worked my hand under her blouse while we were kissing. Then to her back where I discovered...for the very first time and much to my dismay...BRA HOOKS!!! Not one bra hook. Not two bra hooks. But THREE BRA HOOKS!!! Who in the hell invented these? Ironically, I'll bet it was a man. And why in the hell are they in BACK??!!!

I was amazed at how I was somehow keeping this progressing. I mean...unhooking a girl's bra while playing tonsil hockey is no small feat...especially for a greenhorn 15 year old. Then...one clasp let go. Then a second. Finally...the third. Bev's bra seemed like a slingshot!! AND THEN...her pendulous mounds of quivering flesh fell out of their restraints and into my awaiting, hungry hands!!! Sort of. Big lesson here in this elegant Dallas hotel room for Ricky Brown. Life isn't how Ian Fleming describes it. Beverly was a real almost a woman from a real Iowa. And her breasts? Real. Honest. Beautiful. Soft. Firm. Real. I knew this even though my eyes never saw them.

I don't know whether it was shock from Bev's bra seemingly "flying off" after hook # 3 was undone...or the uncharted territory that made me panic. Again...yeah again...I RAN to the door...flung it open and asked a now amused yet frustrated vacuumer "You ARE NOT COMING IN HERE RIGHT?!!!" She shook her head no. And when I returned again to my most patient love/lust interest...began kissing...and moved my hand under her blouse...I realized somehow she had taken her bra OFF!!! It wasn't anywhere to be found. I was dumbfounded. It took me what seemed to be half an hour unfastening it and in the time it took for me to rush to the door and again make a fool of myself Ms. Beverly had made it miraculously disappear. I was amazed. Almost a woman indeed.

As the afternoon waned Bev began running her fingers through my hair. This too was a first for me. I had yet to discover the magic of long, curly hair. It was strictly forbidden for a boy to have long hair and I hated my short unruly mop. But Beverly loved it. And she looked deeply into my eyes while she played with my hair. I was mesmerized. I am to this day still smitten when I hearken back to this memory. My anxiety melted away at that point. Safe at 2nd base. I was in love. It was the summer for it.

Beverly and I wrote back and forth...long letters...for almost 4 years after that coming of age afternoon. We vowed we would meet again. And of course, we never did...eventually fixing my flat feet firmly on the ground. But that afternoon of adolescent abandonment...with a girl who was almost 18 and didn't care that I was a neurotic, clumsy boy...will always bring a smile to my face. Sometimes I hear myself thinking "You're not COMING IN HERE ARE YOU??!!!" And I laugh out loud.

1967. It really *was* the Summer of Love.

Pompeii and the Duck

I'm not certain exactly *what* Pompeii was really. Mostly German Shepherd I believe. I do remember he was always bedraggled. You see, Pompeii was what some people call "an outside dog". Farmers have outside dogs mostly. So it was a little unusual for my "second family"...the Shylos...to have one in the jurisdiction of our small hometown. Still, Pompeii was an incredibly happy hound. And it wasn't like he wasn't *allowed* in the house. Any time he wanted he could come in. I assume he preferred being an outsider...a wanderer...a rebel. He'd be gone for days sometimes only to return again...tail waggin'...crotch sniffin'. Perhaps Pompeii was aware some dogs were chained to their doghouses...or confined to pens...and felt lucky. Maybe he'd witnessed that in his travels. He did seem to have an air of wisdom about him. He knew the street. He knew people. But unlike most...he knew himself.

One summer...and Pompeii was quite old by now...my buddy Doug Shylo and I spent an evening at "Homecoming". This wasn't the usual high school variety. Our town, Olmsted Falls, had a traditional long weekend celebration every year for people to come back to where they grew up. There were rides and baked goods and games and small town festivities and friends. And there always seemed to be a ring toss booth. But this year it had a twist. If you threw a ring over a baby duckling's head you won...a BABY DUCKLING!!. Being boys around the age of 12 or so, Doug and I both believed this was the coolest of cools. Doug won one duckling. I was awarded two.

Of course our parents weren't quite so sure this was the coolest of cools. Yet baby ducklings are so adorable that our bathtub soon became Daffy and Daphne's temporary home. The Shylos on the other hand were a little more pragmatic. After all...if Pompeii stayed outside so would the duck. And if they named the duck I sure don't remember what his name was. I think we all referred to him simply as "Duck".

Baby ducklings do not stay babies for long. Soon enough they are ACK - ing and quacking around our fenced in backyard with the dog and cats. The dog kept her distance...for good reason. Grown ducks are surly at best. Mean even. Hell...they chased the cats around! They pooped everywhere! And a duck won't think twice about biting you either. At an "under the stars" sleepover at Doug's that fall, our buddy Craig woke up screaming when "Duck" bit him viscously on the lip. And the poor kid's lip swelled big enough that it was difficult understanding what he was trying to say. "Faaa Faa FLAA!!" The rest of us got a huge laugh out of the whole thing. But I soon learned to hate ducks as well...especially the two stalking my backyard. Apparently my father wasn't too fond of Daffy and Daphne either. They "disappeared" one day. I think they ended up in the "kidnapper's" freezer.

Pompeii however, saw things differently. He and Duck bonded...became the best of pals. After a long, arduous journey Pompeii would rest under a tree while Duck would cuddle on one of his back haunches and pull burrs out of his matted fur. Duck would sleep curled up between Pompeii's legs. I even witnessed Duck riding on the dogs' back while he sauntered across the yard seeking out a new power spot. *No one*...not even a Shylo...could approach Pompeii without Duck's permission. And the dog protected his fowl friend, as only a loyal canine is capable. This was an amazing relationship to witness. You had to see it to understand the breadth of the connection...the loyalty...the friendship.

One day right before the beginning of winter...right before Thanksgiving...Duck wandered onto Lewis Road. Not a busy thoroughfare. Just busy enough I suppose. You see...Pompeii knew the street. Apparently Duck did not. The school bus ran over Duck killing him instantly. No one thought much about the event...except Pompeii. The grieving dog wandered off as he did many times through the years. But this time Pompeii never came home.

It is not unusual for a dog...or a lot of animals for that matter...to know they are dying,...that this is the time to go find a place to lay and let it be. Most would say Pompeii instinctually did the same.

As for me? It's the unusual bonds...the unexplainable relationships...the surprises in this life I admire and celebrate.

I knew Pompeii.

And I believe he died of a broken heart.

Sandy

When I was a very young boy...5 or 6...we had a tan and white Cocker Spaniel named Sandy. I'm not sure exactly when he became a member of the Brown family...or whose idea it was to get him. After all, my mother was already home with 4 kids under the age of 6. Still...it could very well have been her idea. What's one dog when you already have a house full of four screaming kids? And of course she got stuck with the feeding and general care of the dog...most mothers...especially in 1957 did. Perhaps we weren't typical...poor...four kids...HEY! Let's get another mouth to feed! However it came to pass, my earliest memories include a playful dog we lovingly called Sandy.

Now if you've never been around a Cocker Spaniel before let me tell you about it. Sandy LOVED to bark. We had a big fenced in yard and when we weren't trying to get him into our inflatable wading pool with us...the pool my dad would hyperventilate blowing up...then Sandy would either bite or poke with a claw so dad would have to patch it and blow up again...you could find Sandy running back and forth along the front of the fence barking ferociously at passing cars. He wore paths along the fence. He was that dedicated. Of course since we were all so small, we did spend considerable time playing with our doggie friend.

My mother used to tell this story about how Sandy once bit my youngest brother Don...only my sister Kathy was younger. And mom would proudly exclaim, "So Donny BIT HIM BACK!!" Even as a small child I felt as if my mom was mythologizing the tale. Knowing my brother as I did at the time...and still do...I theorized that Sandy was probably minding his own business when Donny waddled up to the dog and bit him FIRST! However it happened, the story came from my mother and that was that. There apparently were no witnesses.

Sandy was with us constantly. Even when we weren't playing *together*, we were all out in the backyard playing while the pooch raced back and forth on either side of the house along the fence, yelping as if he were chasing the Devil himself away from us. And as with every dog after him...when he got real bored...especially if the four of us other pack members weren't around...he would sneak out of the fence. About 15 minutes later he would slink back into the yard with one of the chickens from a coop a couple houses down the street. Much to our chagrin

Sandy was not bringing a chicken home to play with. It was more like a trip to Doggie Kentucky Fried Chicken...without all the breading and grease. But despite his dog-ness everyone in our family...including my father...looked at him as a member of the family. "You can't have dogs AND furniture." my dad would say. (He said the same of children.) But we all loved Sandy more than any sofa that's for sure. He watched TV with us...so to speak...slept in our beds...ate our food (along with his own.)

One time Sandy tried to go down the basement stairs. We lived in an old farmhouse. The basement had a dirt floor and quarry stone walls. He fell and broke his leg. And even though we were poor my parents took him to the vet. He came home with a cast on his leg...a rounded metal rod poked out from under the plaster...beneath his paw so he wouldn't put weight on it while it healed. I can still remember vividly all of us kids charging into the kitchen...Sandy right on our heals...and when he hit the linoleum with that metal brace he went sprawling on his chest...then jumped up...wagged his tail and begged for something. Sandy knew he had it good. And we thought the same at the time.

On a very hot, humid summer day Sandy was chasing cars back and forth along the fence when he slipped a disc in his spine. He couldn't walk…just dragged his back legs behind him. My father took him to see the vet. A couple hours later he brought him home. The vet told him there was nothing he could do. They had no surgery for animals for things such as this back then. But there was a glimmer of hope. We were to put Sandy on the back porch in a kid's playpen. Apparently, on rare occasion a disc will slip back into place. At least that's what we were told.

We all hoped for the best. But it was extremely hot. And Sandy was miserable. Flies buzzed around the poor dog as if he were no longer amongst the living. None of us wanted to think what we inevitably were thinking. Than one day Sandy bit my Dad…and it became obvious that this was no longer the Sandy who playfully bit holes into our inflatable wading pool. My father got a tarp out of the garage and…after we said our tearful goodbyes…wrapped our playmate carefully in it. He gently placed Sandy in the backseat of our old Ford.

My mom, brothers and sister filed into the house in silence. I stayed to watch the car leave. As I stood there alongside the house I'm sure my father assumed we were all inside. I looked past the windshield and saw my father…this gruff cantankerous man…crying like a baby. I had never seen him cry before. His heart was breaking and so was mine. The scene didn't last long...but it's burnt into my brain. The heat of summer. The suffering of Sandy. The pain in our hearts.

Upon his return we carefully put Sandy's lifeless but peaceful body into a burlap bag and took him out to an apple tree at the beginning of the orchard. Beneath it we dug a hole...said more goodbyes...and covered him over. My father painted a large rock with silver paint. It was the only color he had at the time. And after it dried we put it at the head of Sandy's grave with the notion of putting his name on it at a later date. That never happened. Life goes on. We knew it was Sandy.

Every once in a while I would just go stand over that silver rock. Even after I went to college sometimes I would go back there and just think about my childhood...this yapping Cocker Spaniel...and my family. About the bliss life can provide if you let it...and the inevitable for all living creatures. I saw my father cry only once more in my lifetime. That was the day he looked down at my mother on her deathbed and spoke these words. "I love you. We were poor...but we had fun." And he cried.

Early on in our family life...Sandy was the big reason we had fun.

Seven Minutes...Forty Seconds

Corporal punishment was a given at the public
school I attended for 12 years. Paddling...as it was
known...was an accepted part of school culture. Call it
what you like..."getting paddled"..."swatted"...or even
"cracked" were code phrases for a teacher hitting you
on the ass with a board. Some teachers actually
relished the activity. I had a math teacher...who was
also my track coach...who hung his "paddle" from a
hook at the front of the classroom. He even had a
name for it...although it escapes me now. Some
wielded paddles for discipline...some for kicks.
Others resorted to it because they had no idea how to
control a room full of 14 year olds.
    I didn't mind getting paddled if I felt I had
provoked it and probably deserved it. But once I had
a homeroom teacher paddle me for forgetting to have
my mother sign some form I took home. I call that
"cruel and unusual" punishment. I resent that guy to
this very day. And a guy like the aforementioned
math teacher/track coach...well he ENJOYED doing it.

One day Dave ...who sat directly in front of me...turned around and said something to me. Mr. Winters (he was a very bleak math teacher/track coach) seized the opportunity and called us to the front of the classroom. I kept my mouth shut. Dave whined...the worst thing he could have done. Of course we didn't deserve to get hit with a board for what we had done...but he was just making it worse for himself. I resigned myself to the inevitability. I got hit. Dave got creamed.

Dave was my favorite "cohort in crime". I had a very philosophical view of disrupting a class and Dave did too. I mean any fool can be disruptive...but if you are creative about it...and possibly funny enough to get the class and possibly the teacher to laugh...that was my goal. We both had a sort of surreal deconstructive view of being smart asses. Quality disruption came only when something totally absurd shattered the normal. Dave knew this. It's not like we sat around discussing the fine points of class clowndom (which would have made the Mr. Winter's story more intriguing if in fact this was what he turned around to speak to me about...but it's not so). Dave would say something completely ridiculous and totally out of context...and I would always think it quite hilarious.

For example...there was a laundry detergent on the

market back then called Fab. There was a commercial on television touting the fact that they had added "borax" to make a good detergent even greater. And they had this stupid commercial where stupid people would say (in a very stupid way) "Borax in new Fab?" as a question and…at the same time…giving the question this lilting quality with their voices. "Borax in new Fab?" I can still hear it. One day in Mr. Rinehart's science class (yes THAT Mr. Rinehart…the one who could not control a class to save his life!) Rinehart is up in front droning on about some scientific pap when…out of the blue…in a very ventriliquistic fashion…Dave lets out an oh-so-sincere, "Borax in new Fab?" Everyone burst out laughing. Mr. Rinehart had no idea where this came from or what it meant. It was classic Dave, I still crack up thinking about it. His REAL forte was the racecar. You know that sound racecars make when then screaming around an oval track?

NEEEEOOWWW!! Or he'd whip out an entire race during a lecture.

NeeeEEEOOOOWWW!! ReeeEEOW!! Neow! NEOW! REEOW!! And of course whenever he overdid it with the racecar enthusiasm and Mr. Rinehart realized who it was he would…you guessed it…get paddled.

There were times when I was a smart ass inadvertently. Every month we were supposed to bring in an article involving science, stand up front, and share with the class. This one time I cut out what I believed to be a science article and in my haste neglected to notice the tiny "paid advertisement" written above the so called "article." I strolled up to the front of the room and began to share with the entire class the new scientific breakthrough in the "treatment of painful, itching hemorrhoids". I honestly had no idea what a hemorrhoid was...and I sincerely wish I still didn't. The class began tittering. I persevered in my ignorance...explaining that this new breakthrough would change life, as we knew it.

"That's quite enough Brown" Mr. Rinehart interjected.

"But I'm not finished." I yelped.

"I SAID...that's ENOUGH Brown!"

"Borax in new Fab?" floated up from the back of the room.

Poor Mr. Rinehart. Kids who weren't half as creative (read: cruel) as Dave and I would reek havoc on his class. Sometimes a group of guys would stand in a line all facing the same direction...one hand placed on the shoulder of the boy in front of him...and while whistling the theme from "Bridge Over the River Kwai" would march up to the bulletin board and tear whatever was up there down. Then there would be a "mass paddling" in front of the remainder of the class. In the eighth grade we had a contest to see who could get paddled the most times. The winner would be the guy with the most "cracks". Fellow rapscallions Don and Kenny surpassed me the final day of school by getting three "cracks" each. Their crime? They had no socks on. It was like a felony not to wear socks with one's penny loafers...or Beatle boots.

One ongoing event in Mr. Rinehart's class was known as the "Pencil Sharpening Record". It was a contest to see who could stand at the pencil sharpener sharpening their pencils for the longest duration of time. The record was 5 minutes the day I decided to try to break it. I didn't even HAVE a pencil. I snuck up to the pencil sharpener...which was right by the torn down bulletin board...and began to pretend I was sharpening my pen. Two minutes went by. Rinehart was oblivious to me. Four minutes went by. Crank, crank, crank. I surpassed the five-minute mark!! I had the record!! I was determined to set a new UNBREAKABLE pencil sharpening record!! Six minutes ticked by....SEVEN MINUTES!!!!!!!! Then...at exactly 7 minutes and 40 seconds I heard Mr. Rinehart's booming voice. "Come here and SHOW me that pencil Brown!! NOW!!"

I timidly made my way over to an angry teacher's side. "Let me see that PENCIL!!!" I held my pen in one hand…cupped my other hand over the top of it and proceeded to give Mr. Rinehart a short "peek" at it…a little "smart ass peek-a-boo" if you will. This ENRAGED Mr. Rinehart!! His face swelled up with blood and turned as red as a fire truck. Then he grabbed me by both shoulders and began shaking me violently while he SCREAMED at the top of his lungs "Brown you DUMB HEAD!!! You are a DUMB HEAD BROWN!!!" (Why he could never come up with anything better than "dumb head" is beyond me.) This went on for what seemed to be several minutes. The class was dumbfounded. A dumb head being shaken silly in front of a dumbfounded crowd. When he finished flopping me around like a rag doll I looked directly at him…smiled…and quipped, "Hey! Thanks for the FREE RIDE!" The class roared in approval…but a strange calmness overtook Mr. Rinehart. He smiled back at me with this evil little grin. Then he pointed a finger in my direction…curled it and softly said, "C'mere Brownie." Uh oh. Brownie. I knew it was big trouble when he called me that.

Mr. Rinehart had a very unique paddle at the time. It was round…about 14 inches in diameter…and had 1 inch holes drilled through it. Holes about the size of pepperoni slices. We called it the "pizza paddle". He grabbed his pizza paddle and told me to bend over. I did what he said. "Smart Ass Theater" was over for the day. He only hit me once. Oh...he planned to hit me more than that...but the pizza paddle broke into two pieces (slices?). He looked genuinely disappointed and reluctantly told me to take my seat. But I couldn't sit down...for a week. I had welts on my butt the size of...well...pepperoni slices. I was paddled more than once again after that. I mean...we were having a CONTEST right? Finishing the year with 22 "cracks" and ending up in second place was a real drag. Because...to be honest with you...I think this "crack" should have counted for more than one. It's the one I can still feel when I think about it. Yet it's safe to say corporal punishment probably didn't alter my behavior one way or another. And as far as I know...7 minutes...40 seconds...is STILL the all time pencil sharpening record. And I did it with a pen.

   "Borax in new Fab?
NeeeeEEEEEEOOOOOWWW!!!!!!!!!!"

Our Mister Sun

I remember when I was in elementary school there were these assemblies where the authorities would show this movie titled, "Our Mister Sun". It was about this young, hungry newspaper reporter looking for a scoop and he just happens to end up in the laboratory of one, Doctor Research. I don't recall this reporter's name...perhaps it was Reporter Scoop. That sounds silly enough to be the case. Anyway, there wasn't much of a plot in the film beyond Doc Research yakking on and on...scientifically of course...about how we would all be in dire straights if it weren't for good old Mister Sun. Reporter Scoop, obviously impressed with Doc Research's vast knowledge of our big star, would stand there scribbling furiously in his official looking little notebook "oohing" and "ahhing" in awed respect. And of course there was an ever so lovable cartoon character representing...in an ever so lovable way...the honorable Our Mister Sun. Actually, it wasn't a bad movie...until about the 17th time you saw it. "Our Mister Sun" followed me through at least four grades.

Then there was the sequel. (Why is there ALWAYS a sequel?) This was a God-awful flick called "Hemo the Magnificent" which was about hemoglobin. An entire friggin' movie about hemoglobin. Sure...there was the always charming Doctor Research and that whacky young Reporter Scoop...but an animated hemoglobin just doesn't have the star quality of "Our Mister Sun". Maybe they should have made a sequel about "Some One Else's Mister Sun"...or "Our Mister Uranus"...or perhaps an arty film about a recently divorced...yet still vibrant "Our Ms. Sun". There was very little magnificent about Hemo.

The only copy of "Our Mister Sun" that my school possessed came to an untimely demise when I was in the eighth grade. The science teacher...and I use the term quite loosely...Mr. Rinehart ("Our Mister Rinehart"?)...who was notorious for his inability to control his class (We called him Otis after the town drunk on the Andy Griffith show...which may have been unfair to Otis.) was showing it one day in class. I assume Mr. Rinehart either had no lesson planned that day or he merely wanted to take refuge in the possibility of "Our Mister Sun" keeping us under some sort of control. Given the fact most of us had seen this movie at least 10 or 12 times this was obviously the fantasy of a broken man. And this was right at the beginning of my life long quest of railing against authority...ALL authority...ANY authority. After the film was over he fixed it up on the projector so that it could be rewound. This was LONG before the advent of videotape so film had to be run backwards at breakneck speed in order for it to be rewound on the original spool. Anyway...the plug for the projector was a little on the shaky side so Rinehart mistakenly asked ME to make sure it didn't fall out of the wall outlet. So I'm standing there watching this plug bored out of my fourteen year old mind with the projector whirring and rewinding, whirring and rewinding when...on a whim...I YANKED the plug OUT of the electrical socket and immediately rammed it back INTO the electrical outlet! What happened next was a big physics lesson for the entire class.

The rewinding film slowed...then stopped momentarily...then abruptly yanked back into fast rewind mode thus SNAPPING the film in half!!! So now instead of it being rewound on to its reel, film was SPEWING all over the floor in a quite delightful Dionysian suicide dance. Of course all my classmates were laughing their collective asses off while Mr. Rinehart chased me around the room yelling, "Brown you DUMB HEAD! You DUMB HEAD". (Geez...I'm reeking havoc here and all he can come up with is "Dumb Head"?) It took him at least THREE laps around the room before he thought it might be a good idea to stop the carnage of "Our Mister Sun". The film was never to my knowledge shown again. I suppose it could have been repaired...but it would have taken a good three weeks to rewind the film by hand...back onto the reel before attempting to repair it.

For the big adventure, Mr. Rinehart beat my ass with a paddle not once...but THREE times. (This was always his lame attempt a controlling the boys.) I don't think I sat down for a week. I guess sometimes you've got to make sacrifices for the sake of entertainment. My only regret is that I did this to "Our Mister Sun" and not "Hemo the Magnificent". Perhaps this makes me living proof that corporal punishment rarely...if at all...works. And I'd like to think that whacky young Reporter Scoop would have enjoyed the scene.

If You're Happy and You Know It

A lot of kids at the tender age of 18 leave home for college...if they aren't runaways...or back then...draft dodgers. And while university *was* my general direction for the fall of 1970, this summer was my first of four as a camp counselor. It was a Lutheran camp...still is...about 20 miles south of Youngstown. Nestled between Turkey Run and Bull Creek...along route 154...between Rogers and Negley...this was my first foray into rural Ohio...also my first time away from home. I never looked back.

I used to joke that you had to be UGLY to live in NEGLEY! And...for the most part...that was pretty much the case. That's one of the things I learned early on in the experience. There wasn't much intellectual stimulation...and most people weren't pretty. Some were nice enough, but definitely not much to look at...especially in Negley. Probably the second epiphany I had was that out in the woods...and this camp was primitive (I lived in a teepee for 3 of 4 summers) a young man could get...well...how shall I put this...uh...a trifle *randy* at times. Horny if you will.

Most of the campers who stayed at Camp Frederick came for a week at a time for what was called "catechism camp". Catechism...in the Lutheran sense at least...is where you go to class and memorize what you believe. This really struck me when I was in catechism. "Wow! I'm MEMORIZING what I BELIEVE!!" This seemed more than a little disconcerting to me at the time. I mean...shouldn't there be some journey involved to enlightenment? But I didn't make a fuss and got confirmed...which is the Lutheran version of graduating from high school.

So all these 13 and 14 year old kids came for a week of "confirmation camp"...a new group every week...maybe 30 or 35 total...with their pastors to memorize what they believed. And the majority of them were girls. This is when it became painfully obvious to my 18 year old brain...as well as other parts of my anatomy...that it was true...girls did "mature" at a faster rate than boys. Some MUCH FASTER indeed. What made this situation all the more difficult (I refrain from using "harder" as the adjective here) was that some of these 14 year old girls were quite aware of this...and knew how to use it to their advantage.

Here's an example for your enjoyment. The first summer, Camp Frederick had no swimming pool. Everybody swam in the swimming hole...where the two aforementioned creeks converged. How the hell we got away with this is a miracle in itself. I guess no parents thought to call the health department. I mean...it was fun...Tarzan rope and all...but still. By the next summer a concrete "dish" had been poured...in ground like a pool...but was still filled with water from the creeks. Again...how the hell we got away with this I'll never know. Anyway, one day I'm pumping water from the creeks into the "pool" and a pretty, young, 14 year old girl who...as my Uncle Gene would say...was blossoming quite early (and often) sauntered up close to me. She was wearing nothing but cut off shorts and a tight t-shirt. I'm standing there shooting water into the "pool" when she looks up at me, cocks her head just so, and purrs "Work your *hose Rick*!!"...giving me a wry smile at the word "hose". This did my emotional stability at the time no good whatsoever.

By summer number two...the "pool with creek water in it" summer...Camp Frederick was drawing enough campers to warrant a "junior staff" which was comprised of 3...maybe 4...high schoolers. One of the guys...Steve...he and I got to be buds. I suppose I was like a big brother to him. And he and I both played guitar. We were the best guitar players at the camp...which isn't saying a whole hell of a lot. I swear...to qualify for camp guitarist all you had to do was own a guitar and have two arms. Church and camp is where I learned to play real loud...to drown out the people who had no business having a guitar around their necks. Steve and I could play chords above the first position...and since most camp songs of this era had like 1 and ½ chords and 47 verses...well...we amazed people...which wasn't difficult by any means.

And as far as the 14 year old "hose teases" were concerned...for 17 year old Steve they were a nuisance...trouble at the worst. But for 20 year old Rick...they were *jailbait...hard time* maybe.

So Steve and I played guitars at all our campfires. Now the key to playing guitar at a campfire is this: play all the more difficult songs first. Why you might ask? Because the fire is huge at the beginning but continues to die down...it gets darker... and you can't see much of anything for the closing...hand holding "Kumbaya". That tune only has three chords so it's not an issue...which is good because on a dark night by the time you get to this song your hands might be oblivious to you.

To make campfires more interesting Steve and I tried to inject a little secularism. I had learned this song from a college boy on a bus ride to a Luther League convention in Dallas in 1967. (That excursion is a story for another day.) Anyway, it was called "Salvation Army". Everyone would make up verses. We had a contest every week to see who could come up with the best new verse. Some of the better ones went like this. The leader would shout "There's only one bar in town". Then everyone would boo real loud. And the leader would yell "But it's 10 miles long!!" Everyone would cheer and immediately sing:

"Salvation Army, Salvation Army!
Put a nickel in the drum
Save another drunken bum.
Salvation Army, Salvation Army!
Put a nickel in the drum and you'll be saved!!"

Some of the other great verses were:
"All the barmaids wear grass skirts!"
"Booooooooooooo!"
"They hand out lawnmowers at the door!!"
"Yaaaaaaaaaay!!!!!!!!!"

"Salvation Army, Salvation Army...etc."
And:
"The bar's doors are closed at midnight!"
"Boooooooooo!!"
"The windows are open ALL NIGHT!!!"
"Yaaaaaaaaaaay!!!"

Forget the swimming hole...how the hell did we get away with THIS?!!

One day, when Steve and I were both feeling like we were stuck in the woods with a bunch of babes in the woods (read: horny) some of which were most definitely "hose teases" we came up with a way to get back at them. There was this song we both hated to play. It was a children's song really and it was called "If You're Happy and You know It". Typical three chord, monotonous Bible School tune that we were pretty much required to play. Ironically, it was structured much like "Salvation Army". It went like this:

"If you're happy and you know it clap your hands!
If you're happy and you know it clap your hands!
If you're happy and you know it and you really want to show it
If you're happy and you know it clap your hands!"

Of course you'd clap your hands at the end of each line. In subsequent verses you would sing "stamp your feet" (stomp feet)...then "shout Amen! (shout Amen)" and of course for the last verse you sang "If you're happy and you know it do all three" (clap, stomp AND shout Amen!). Clever huh? You can probably see why this tormented us so. At least we were playing guitars so we wouldn't actually have to participate at the highest level. But we came up with a colossal...no...*brilliant* verse of our own...one for all the "hose teases" out there at the campfire. It went like this:

"If you're happy and you know it touch your elbows behind your back!
If you're happy and you know it touch your elbows behind your back!
If you're happy and you know it and you really want to show it if you're happy and
you know it touch your elbows behind your back!!!"
Steve and I ALWAYS requested this one early on in the campfire...when it was still pretty light...before dusk...so we could enjoy all the girls attempting to touch their elbows behind their backs. Of course...being a grown man and all...I tried my darndest to observe the women counselors. But every once in a while I'd sneak a peak at one of the "hose teases". Just to see how quickly she was blossoming...and give her a wry smile of my own.
And the beauty of it all...beyond the leering I mean...is that...to the best of my knowledge...no one ever caught on. Not even the female counselors.
Disclaimer: the author strongly advises readers *not* to try this in Negley.

How I Spent My (Very First) Summer Vacation

It was late August 1972 and my third summer at a
Lutheran camp named Frederick about 25 miles
south of Youngstown, Ohio. Hardly the garden spot of
the U.S. but pleasant enough. And for about the last
month or so I had pressed my buddy Steve to take a
trip with me. Considering I was pulling in about 400
bucks for the summer...he even less...this was not an
easy sell. But I finally convinced him...and his
father...that my 1963 Chrysler
Newport...affectionately named Smiley...was up to
the task. I also conned my brother Don into coming
along for the adventure. The fact that at the ripe old
age of 20, I was taking two minors across state lines
never occurred to me...until I sat down to spin this
yarn.

Smiley was the largest car I've ever owned...and
that includes a couple Jeep Cherokees and a 1964 VW
microbus. The 4- door, big white whale was so
spacious I could literally open a back door and toss
my bicycle in the backseat without hitting the door
on the other side of the vehicle. The car I drive
now...a Miata...would have fit into the trunk. And I

don't remember...but it probably got 8 miles to the gallon. But in 1972 the price of gas was probably 30 cents a gallon or so. The speed limit...at least in Ohio...was 70 mph. This was in that blissfully ignorant time of gas guzzling monsters that abruptly came to an end not soon afterward. So I had all the confidence in the world in my big boat with the push button transmission on the dashboard. At least I convinced Steve and Don I did.

In preparation for our very first vacation sans parents I approached my Uncle Andy...who really wasn't my uncle at all but a very good friend of my family and fishing buddy to my dad and crazy brother Jim. I figured him being an outdoorsman and all...well...he could give me some valuable pointers. And this is what he told me to do. Buy a big cooked ham...say 5 or 7 pounds...put it in a cooler with some ice. And whenever the three of us got hungry...and I'm quoting here...just "rip off a big ole piece!!!" Amazingly this sounded like a good plan to me. That's exactly what I did. Besides a camp stove for making breakfast...usually consisting of one HUGE pancake (for some reason I thought this quite hilarious)...we banked on our ham for daily sustenance. It's incredible how moronic you can be when you're young.

So bright and early on Thursday, August 24, 1972

Don, Steve and I piled into Smiley...me behind the wheel. "Uh...where exactly are we going" Steve inquired. It hadn't dawned on any of us to plan a destination. Assuming the "adult in charge" role I stammered, "Mmmmmmmmmm...the *BASEBALL HALL OF FAME!!!!*" This was the first thing to pop into my head and I'd always wanted to go there. Don and Steve didn't protest. And of course being the purist that I am, I decided we should properly "see America" and take only back roads. Soon a '63 Chrysler Newport filled with camping equipment, three long haired hippy types and a big ass ham on ice began venturing across northern Pennsylvania into New York. The adventure had begun!!

After a hasty tour of the Baseball Hall of Fame in Cooperstown we ended up some 560 miles from our start, camping in the Catskill Mountains. Except for the quick tour and a few stops at gas stations to ask about the hissing power steering unit (we got opinions ranging from a broken head gasket to a guy who said not to worry about it after he squeezed a small rock into the bracket...we went with his diagnosis) we had spent all day in the car. We got up the next morning determined to drive some more. "Now where are we going?" Don asked. "Mmmmmmmmmm...*Cape Cod*!!" I exclaimed once again striving to sound somewhat authoritative. And after the 560 miles on the back roads we'd all seen enough of America to take the freeway now. Yet before we hit the highway we managed to stop for lunch in Woodstock, New York. And while it wasn't the scene of the rock festival...it IS where Dylan once lived and was a lovely artists' community.

Coming in to the Boston area we witnessed a sobering sight. Across the highway a convertible...with its top down...heading the opposite direction careened into the median and flipped over crushing the windshield flat. I assumed the passengers had a similar fate and I caught myself hoping no one survived...for their sake. All three of us were stunned and drove the rest of the way to the western end of Cape Cod in silence. I still have vivid flashbacks of that scene occasionally...especially when driving with *my* top down. We had plenty of time to ponder it too once we got in the huge traffic jam. It was rush hour on a Friday in August and people were headed to the cape just like us...except most of them probably had a place to stay.

After sitting in traffic for what seemed like eternity we spent the good part of the early evening trying to find a campground. But everywhere was booked solid. While looking out over the Atlantic at a tourist welcome center, throwing back pop (don't you mean sodas?), while savoring a "big ole piece a ham" a stranger gave us advice.

"You got sleepin' bags right? Just sleep in the dunes!!! God's country! It's the beach and it's FREE boys!!" Something like that. It wasn't good advice. We took it because...well...we really had no recourse. And that night was a classic case of romance meets reality. First there was a foghorn from hell...followed by Don freaking out because he thought he heard a rattlesnake (While I reassured him there were no such reptiles in Massachusetts I really had no clue.)...followed by sand flees and mosquitoes. All that with the horrible accident fresh in our minds.

We did manage to score a camp site the next day in Provincetown. It was a piece of ground barely large enough for a pup tent...picnic table...1963 Chrysler Newport...and the scruffiest white pine I'd ever seen. It felt like the Hilton after the previous night of freedom in the dunes. And cruising around Provincetown...on foot of course...was an eye opening experience. Gay people...were everywhere!! Or so it seemed to the three long hairs from oh so sophisticated Ohio. And they were pleasant...*normal* even. Epiphanies like this happened every time I ventured out of my little Lutheran college/little Lutheran camp bubble. It was quite exhilarating really. People were reveling in their secularism...seemingly without a care.

After a couple nights on the cape we headed toward Boston. And we must have enjoyed driving through the city. We did it four times!!! Boston is a horrible place to drive. At least back then, I had a tank of a car to defend myself with. So to calm our nerves...mine in particular...we decided to take in some history. So we stopped to look at Plymouth Rock. And gazing down at it I thought, "It's just a frikkin' ROCK!!! Might not even be the right goddamned ROCK!!!" Being a history major in college I took this presumptuous "landmark" personally. At least...like sleeping in the sand dune...it was free. Looking at a rock should always be free of charge. I don't care what the hell rock it is.

So the three of us just headed north...seemed like as good a direction as any. And we stumbled upon another cape...this one called Ann. What a lovely discovery Cape Ann was...and still is I suppose. Rockport...with its artist colony...is located there. And for a little more salt of the earth local color there's Gloucester, where fishing boats bring their catch in daily during the season. I fell in love with Cape Ann. This is where Don, Steve and I all finally relaxed. We celebrated by ditching the now tiresome...and greening...big ass ham...for a much more joyous feast. Quart bottles of pop and a box of Fudgesicles!!! After three days of big ole hunks a ham this was quite the feast indeed. Hey...we were in the land of the first Thanksgiving and we could think of no better way to show our respect!!

And there was...and still is...a beautiful campground where we could chill out in spacious campsites. Cape Ann Campground (but of course) is a place I have returned to on at least three occasions. The beaches...especially Good Harbor...are beautiful. This was indeed heaven compared to the frantic frazzled pace of the previous days. We reveled as long as time and our limited resources allowed. I made the biggest pancake yet for breakfast!! We swam in the Atlantic. Reclined in the sun. Recharged our friendships with each other.

We thought the drive home would take us two days. But that was because of the "back roads" tedium of day one. So after we stopped at a god awful place called Nu-Look Campground...something like that...somewhere in New York I think...we decided nothing could be better than what we had left behind on Cape Ann. So we repacked Smiley and drove home...dumping what was left of our now green big ass ham along the way. What a great trip it was. Commradery...adventure...sun...sea and a banquet of pop and Fudgesicles!!! And my apologies to Uncle Andy...who wasn't really my uncle at all. But it will be a cold day in hell the next time I "rip off a big ole piece" of ham from a cooler.

The Non-Fiction Theater of the Truly Mundane

proudly presents:

Overdue Notice

Scene: A street corner in the poor, disheveled section of a medium sized American city. As the curtain rises a 21 year old Rick is seen stage right in the driver's seat of a large, older American car facing the audience. The year is 1973 as reflected in Rick's attire...bell-bottom pants, tie-dyed t-shirt, Black Converse Hi Tops. His hair is very long and parted in the middle. He is wearing wire-rimmed glasses. On the car's seat next to him is a small pile of books. Stage left, standing on the corner is a small group of provocatively dressed women...mini skirts with all the trappings of 1970's fashion decadence. It is a beautiful spring afternoon. The women laugh and carry on.

Rick (pretending to bring the car to a stop at the intersection) – "Shit! I think I'm lost." (To no one in particular.)

One of the women (#1) sees him and strolls suggestively across the street to the car. She is wearing a very short black leather mini skirt, matching leather jacket and thigh high, spike-heeled boots. It takes some time for Rick to notice her (she approaches on the side of his bad eye) but when he does he struggles to contain his composure. The woman smiles confidently, leans onto the car door and sticks her head in the window close to Rick's face.

Woman (#1) (seductively in a whispered tone) – "Hi there *baaayyy beeeeeeeee!* Wanna go *out with meeeee?*" She winks at him.
Rick (who is visibly shaken) – "Uh, well...ordinarily I'd really like that. But...uh...uh...I gotta go to the...uh...library."

Upon hearing this she steps back from the car and puts her hands on her hips with an air of disgust.

Woman – "Say WHAT?!!"

Her companions on the street corner laugh and snicker and point at Rick's car.

Rick – "I'm really sorry...but you see (pointing at the

pile of books next to
him)...they're...they're...*OVERDUE*!!"

Curtain

Cast:

Rick – himself (age 21)
Woman #1 – herself
Woman #2 – herself
Woman #3 – herself
Woman #4 – herself

Remembering Snook

My Dad's nickname was Snook. He got it from one or more of his many brothers and sisters who numbered 10 or 11...I forget. I had an Uncle Skeek. I had an Uncle Mooney. Snook's real name was Richard...like mine...and he went by Dick almost always. Yet my cousins always called him "Uncle Snookie". He didn't much like the moniker...but it stuck like glue.

I won't kid you. The guy was a real pain to live with...demanding...boisterous...your typical blue-collar father. But he was a good father. He came home after work every day. He was hard on us kids...but he loved us. He was hard on my mother...but he loved her. Yet even though he quit high school to join the Navy and go to war he had a certain decency...and wisdom...an intuitiveness that I don't remember seeing in my friends more mild mannered fathers.

He had this sense of humor. He would just start with the dumb jokes until he found one that finally made you laugh. "Hey...you know Fat Burns? Just light a match to it!" "Ever heard of Phil Dirt? He's Sam Spade's brother in law." And then there was my personal favorite. He would say in a very deadpan voice, "You know what BURNS my ass?" Then he would thrust his hand out about waist high and yell, " a FIRE 'bout THIS HIGH!!!" It still cracks me up. And he would do these outrageous things no one else would have the nerve to do. Like when he heard a rumor that the owner of the shop he worked in was moving the place to Texas...whenever the bosses would come around he would start singing, "The stars at night are big and bright" clap, clap, clap, "Deep in the heart of Texas."

Snook did this great imitation of the Pope. He would make the sign of the cross and chant, "Icanbeatanybodyinthishouseindominoes!!" This too still cracks me up! And whenever we drove past a cemetery he would say, "Hard to believe but people are DYING to get into that place!" Religion was a good subject for him. His philosophy for why he attended church regularly? "You're dead a LONG time." I think that's funny...and more honest than most churchgoers.

For a while me, my two brothers, and Snook were custodians at our church. What this means is that you do a lot of work, get paid very little, are appreciated even less and learn that it's the LAWYER who becomes president of the congregation...not the janitor. Still Snook made the best of the situation. I remember the whole family would be getting ready for church, invariably running late and you would see my father frantically brushing the shoulders of his sport coat while shouting downstairs at my poor mother, "GOD DAMNED DOG HAIR!! ANNE! ANNE!" One time we had to get to church really early...way before the minister did. Why? Because Snook left his cigar on the altar. Fortunately it had gone out before he put it there. And then there was the time he put the bowl from the baptismal fount on his head and went into this routine like he was shooting a machine gun! "Rat-tat-tat-tat!"

One time I asked my dad if our ancestors came over on the Mayflower. He told me they did. When I learned later on it wasn't true and confronted him about it he said, "There had to be a Brown in there somewhere. And what the hell difference does it make which boat we came over on? We got here didn't we?" That's the way he was. Seat of your pants, blue-collar truisms that sometimes contradicted each other...but it didn't matter. "You can't make money by workin'" He'd say, "It takes money to make money." Or, "You don't get nothin' for nothin'"...which...I believe is a triple negative...maybe quadruple...but true none the less. On domestic issues it was either, "You can't have dogs AND furniture" or "You can't have KIDS AND furniture" Both of which we all know to be true.

For a while my father had a lawn mower repair shop in the garage out back. I have many fond memories of hanging out there watching him work and listening to baseball on a summer night. Tony DiAngelo from across the street would be bangin' away at a mower with a hammer...which seemed to be the only tool he knew how to use. He worked at a junkyard. Those were good times. Snook had these signs up in the shop. One read "Confucius say, 'No got the cash...no cut the grass." And "Confucius say, "No got the dough...no gonna mow." And my favorite, "Good tools cost money! Maybe mine aren't good but put them back anyway!"

And how he LOVED to watch television. Ironically it brought the family together...because there was only one television. Snook's television. But we all sat around watching "Gunsmoke" and whatever Snook wanted to watch. These are some fond memories. Once...after I had gone off to college, he and my mom were visiting me at school when Snook told me, "Television ain't any good any more Ricky". When I asked him why he replied, "They ran out of PLOTS!!"

So this is the kind of guy he was. But the big thing I learned from him was tolerance. Yes from this belligerent, frustrated man I learned to be tolerant of others. Having served on a ship in the navy during World War II...a subject he almost never spoke of.

He was on a ship that went in after a battle, removed the dead and helped repair the guns. He wasn't proud of this. Once he told me about a friend of his. A black man. In order for Snook to see his friend he had to go to the back of the ship to the galley. Why? Because the cooks were black and they had to be segregated in the galley...away from the white guys. Same navy, same country. One time while we were on a vacation in South Carolina he and I took the car to a garage because the exhaust was falling off. While the car was up on the rack he introduced himself to a man of color there for much the same automotive reason. The man's name was Redd. And Snook said, "Imagine that! A white man named Brown and a black man named Redd." A year later when I had a black friend from Akron, I had met at a youth church function stay at our house Snook insisted we all go to church together...and I remember people walking out.

When I was 12 he bought me my first guitar. We looked at inexpensive guitars first but when he learned they were made in Japan he bought me a Gibson...from the good old USA. "I ain't buyin' no Jap guitar". Yet 7 or 8 years later he bought a Mazda and proclaimed, "Them Japs make good cars Ricky!" I guess he forgave them by then.

Oh sure...I'm romanticizing a little here. I don't miss going out to change the oil in the car on the coldest night of the year after he waited until it was dark. "Put the oil in Rick!' "Does it go here dad?" "NOOOOO...I want you to POUR it all over the engine!" Or when I was going on a date and he didn't like the girl he'd say, "Don't do any thing stupid." I'd say, "Waddya mean." And Snook would yell, "YOU KNOW WHAT I MEAN!" Hey I do not miss those times...funny as they seem now.

After my mom died Snook met a woman and remarried. She was nice enough...but she was a Southern Baptist. So Snook became a Southern Baptist...and believe me...he did not make a good one. At his funeral there was this young minister...one that Snook always joked cared more about taking his money than saving his soul. And if I hadn't written a little biography about my father I never would have known it was his funeral. So this young Baptist minister is up in front of Snook's casket...Bible in hand...arms flailing about...talking about hell and salvation...and I thought to myself, "Hey buddy! Ya know what burns MY ASS? A fire 'bout THIS HIGH!!"

And I swear I saw Snook smile.

The Nick in My Guitar

I have a great guitar. It's a 1972 Guild D-50 that my parent's helped me buy for my 21st birthday. I still own it. I still play it. I try not to get attached to "things" but to tell you the truth I LOVE my guitar. I have other guitars...good instruments all...but I don't love them like I do this Guild D-50.

So back in 73 when I worked out a special program with my college to volunteer at a drop in center for high school kids out in Ventura, California I took it with me. My buddy John who was enrolled at Trinity Lutheran Seminary was serving his year of internship at the center. He played guitar also. He had a Yamaha...which is pretty good...but it's not a Guild. I spent the good part of six weeks in this slow paced (at least at the time) little town some 70 miles north of Los Angeles on the coast. I made a lot of friends. I played a lot of guitar. I couldn't really afford Spring Break. This was better anyway. Six weeks on the west coast and I get credit for a sociology course. The entire month of January, and part of February. I had a wonderful experience. My brother Don and another friend were out there with me, and that made it all the better.

When it came time to return to the snowy landscape of central Ohio...John, my brother and myself decided to make a drive out to the Grand Canyon. Steve was a bit homesick so he flew directly back. The rest of us wanted to squeeze out just a little more time together and do something exciting. We settled on hiking into the Grand Canyon, spending the night, hiking out and driving to Denver where Don and I would board a plane back to Cleveland.

The three of us borrowed John's next door neighbor's new VW Super Beetle. Into this egg shaped auto we managed to pack 3 suitcases, food for a few days, a pair of snow shoes (really) and, of course, my Guild D-50. It took us a good hour just to get everything into this little vehicle. When the three of us finally squeezed into the bug the guy in the back seat had to look through a snowshoe. We took turns. We didn't care. We were young. And being so inexperienced with traveling of course we figured we could drive to the Grand Canyon, spend a night in it, drive to the Rocky Mountains, spend the night camping, drive to Denver the next day, get on a plane and fly home. All this...in about 3 days time. The schedule was tight...to say the least.

We were having a grand old time until we pulled into a tiny burg in Arizona called Kingman. It being the early 70's and all, my brother and I had really long hair and beards. Back then that was enough to have truckers throwing lit cigarettes out of their rigs at you. Ironically, a lot of truckers now days look more like hippies themselves...not to mention Vietnam Veterans. But back then the long hair so enraged people some of them would call you names...or perhaps spit at you.

As soon as we crossed the Arizona state line and drove past the sign for "Kingman, Arizona" I heard the police siren and saw the lights. We were being pulled over for some unknown reason. John was almost having a heart attack. He was driving...and if I had to describe John in a nutshell he was a likable goody two shoes. John was worried.

Two stern looking highway patrolmen...who both had the disposition of a cop on a donut free diet...ordered the three of us out of the car. I was told to "shut up" after asking why we'd been stopped. Then I along with John and Don were each frisked, spread eagle on the hood of the VW in his own turn. When they found nothing on us we were instructed to take everything out of the car...which we did. These two cops (this is NOT the word I would have used at the time) tore apart everything...our suitcases, our packs, our food bags. As the search went on...and it lasted for hours...3 to be exact...it was becoming more and more apparent to these officers that we had nothing on us. Their mood began to take on a more friendly tone...especially after they found out that granola was a mixture of nuts and stuff that we were going to eat while hiking. "What's THIS son?" "Uh...granola sir". "And exactly what is THAT?" "Um...it's a kind of trail mix sir". "Oh." Geez...if I had taken 5 ounces of oregano with me I'd probably STILL be serving time.

After searching everything their attention turned to my guitar case. They tore it open, pulled out my beloved D-50...which I had owned for about 3 months now...and began shaking it violently while holding it upside down. "Nice lookin' git fiddle son." he exclaimed as he shook it. I suppose he was sure I had put a pound of marijuana in there, or some such thing. When he was done having his way with my guitar...while he was putting it back into the case...he slapped the headpiece against a buckle on the case. And when I looked down there it was...a gash about an inch long on the back of the headstock. The cop didn't seem to notice. By this time, knowing we had nothing incriminating we were told they pulled us over because we looked suspicious. Both of them were almost embarrassed by this time. Getting the news over their radio that the car hadn't been stolen...and yes...a dispatcher had talked to the owner...they were downright apologetic. "Gee you guys are one of the few clean stops we've made". This, in no way, made me feel like buying tickets to their Policeman's Ball. I was biting my lip so hard I'm still amazed it's on my face.

We hurried to the Grand Canyon, parked the car, and started down. We didn't have much sunlight left for the day so we hurried. The time was about 4 in the afternoon...in February. It's a 7 mile hike down...11 out. It's much steeper going down. Beat feet was the day's slogan from that point on. We all tried to put what happened in Kingman behind us and enjoy ourselves. After we marveled at the sunset John took out his flashlight. Our ONLY flashlight. Somehow, mysteriously, it had been turned on and the batteries were now completely dead. It was dark. It was February. We had almost five more miles to hike.

My eyesight in the broad daylight...even at the ripe age of 21...wasn't good. Night vision is still more adventure. "Hey Don! Is that the path over there?" "Rick! Come here!" That's the Colorado River." We did find a candle...for whatever THAT'S worth in the middle of the Grand Canyon. I probably didn't realize just how much danger was involved while it was happening. Now I know we all could have been hurt quite badly...possibly killed in a fall. Yet we made it.

Slept overnight, hiked out and eventually made it home. I'm not sure how but we did.

I suppose it would be wrong to blame the cops for turning and leaving on our only flashlight. But why would any of us do this? Perhaps it was inadvertent...I don't know. I really don't care. And I'm not trying to make myself out to be a victim. I knew at the time my long hair and beard and clothes could make these types suspicious. And hey...it makes for an exciting story right? Still...to this very day I blame the cops for the flashlight...whether it was intentional or not doesn't matter to me.

I've thought about this experience a lot since 9/11. Our paternalistic leaders assure me that profiling is necessary for our safety...our security. And I think about how had I been a young African American kid that afternoon what might have conspired. Perhaps we were finally freed because we were white. It seems now if some one gets too dark of a tan they're increasing their chances of being "detained". Labels are back in vogue folks. Terrorists. "They're not soldiers they're TERRORISTS." I'm not by any means implying there are no terrorists. I just don't trust Donald Rumsfeld or Dick Cheney deciding these things. Especially Cheney whose whereabouts and meetings are as clandestine as the Nixon Administration during the early days of Watergate.

"We know what's best for you." Yeah, yeah. I'm sure these two cops knew what was best for Kingman, Arizona too. "The Evil Doers." "The Evil Axis" George W.'s nicknames used to seem so cute...albeit nonsensical.

My guitar is pretty beat up these days. Anyone who has seen me play knows I'm not a gentle guitarist by any means. But those scrapes and cracks and nicks were all put there in the passion of a song...a friendly jam session where perhaps I'd had one too many beers...or a rousing encore. All those abrasions on my 21st birthday Guild D-50 were lovingly put there by ME...with the exception of one. The one on the Guild headstock. And I certainly have no intention of forgetting who put it there.

Mistuh Wick
Part I

During my senior year at college...followed by the first year of my marriage (aka as the "What the hell do I do NOW year) I drove kids to and from school in a Volkswagen Microbus. For those too young to remember the Microbus, suffice it to say it as a van with an air cooled, low horsepower engine in the rear. I was a driver for the Franklin County Crippled Children School. Cripple...when was the last time you heard THAT word? I believe it's simply called Easter Seals now. And my dog Daisy rode with me. The kids LOVED Daisy. My bus was dubbed the "Daisy Bus". But that's a story for another day. The kids were instructed to call me Mr. Rick...and they did.

I had one of the longer routes that took me outside the county. So I got to know these kids pretty well. I still fondly recall many of them. They were after all, just kids. That's how they looked at themselves. There was Chris, a boy born without legs, as well as a mild speech impediment. He had artificial legs the school had made for him. His speech was out of their league I suppose. He would walk with a cane.

Perched atop the prosthetic, ambling through the school's hallways, he looked like a tiny British aristocrat.

Chris hated his legs. He would say to me, "Mistuh Wick...I hate these wegs!" When I asked him why he replied, "Cause I can't wide my Big Wheel with them. But I can sit on the seat without them and use my awrm to cwank the peddle. I can go FAST! Faster than some kids WITH wegs!!" Sometimes when the Microbus would go around a corner Chris's legs would fall over with a thud...and I'd hear "Mistuh Wick!! My WEGS FEWL OVUH!!!" So I'd reassure this little gentleman I would correct the situation at the next stop.

There was Tina...Chris's girlfriend. Tina couldn't talk. She was mute because once her young mother gave her too much aspirin when she was an infant. It burned out something in her brain that affected her speech. Chris loved her all the same. The two of them would sit together directly behind me in the Microbus, Chris's legs standing in front of them, and sing along with the radio. At the time Helen Reddy had a hit that I couldn't stand. Tina and Chris however, loved it. And I could NEVER switch the station before they recognized it. I'd thrust my hand to the radio and change the station only to hear Tina's

"Uh! Uh!" and Chris would politely say, "Mistuh Wick. Pwease put it back on Hewen Weddy!"

I drove a lot of kids born with brain and spinal problems. These are the children you will never, ever see on a poster. They aren't considered cute by most people's standards. And…at least back then…they didn't live to see their 8th birthday. Three of these severely handicapped kids died in the two years I drove them to and from school.

And two kids were autistic. The one boy I heard say a few words to his mother…once. The other boy…Jimmy…said one word. He would look me straight in the eye…his eyes wide and wild…thrust his tiny fist violently into the air and proclaim "GO! GO! GOOOOOOOO!!" He was a boy of few words…but I liked him. He had style.

The very first day I drove this group of kids home from a day at "cripple school" my boss showed me how to put seat belts on…strap in the children in car seats…the ones with the short lives and no chance to be a poster child. Once I had everyone ready I made my way to the driver's seat…fastened my own seat belt…and turned on the radio. I had never done my route before and was more than a little nervous.

"GOOOOOOOOO!!!!!" Jimmy cried from the farthest seat in back. And off we went.

Using my crib notes, I tried to navigate our virgin

journey through neighborhoods as Chris and Tina serenaded us all from the middle of the bus. "Gyspies! Twamps and thieves!!" Chris would sing enthusiastically accompanied by Tina's "Uh! Uhs!". But I was a nervous wreck. And I invariably got lost. A couple times I heard "Mistuh Wick! My wegs fewl ovuh again!!" And I'd stand them upright at the next stop. Why we didn't just decide to lay them down I can't tell you.

As I began to get waaaay over schedule...I mean a driver can't be taking a handicapped kid home at 6 pm when school let out at 3 now can he?... I got a little frantic. Hey...I was 21 years old! Upon realizing I had...once again...missed a turn I whipped the VW Microbus into a driveway. Blam! Chris's legs hit the deck. Then...from the back...again...I heard, "Mistuh Wick!"

"I know Chris. You're legs fell over" I replied.

"It's not my WEGS Mr Wick. It's JIMMY! I think he needs youwr HEWLP!!." I looked to the very back seat. Jimmy was dangling...upside down...hanging in mid air by his seat belt. It probably wasn't...but I swore his face was blue. He had only been that way a minute. Still...I almost panicked. I ran to the back of the little bus...sat Jimmy upright...hugged him and asked him if he was okay.

Jimmy looked up at me...his eyes wide and wild...violently thrust his little fist into the air and proclaimed for all to hear,
"GOOOOOOOOOOOOOOOOOOO!!!!"
And that's what we did.

Gold Circle

Despite the fact it was the tail end of the 1960's, I never did any recreational drugs in high school. I drank a tiny bit but not enough to mention really. Even at college I was pretty upright all the time. Attending a small Lutheran university in the middle of the Midwest did not present the opportunity much. Although after I *did* begin smoking marijuana I occasionally bought it from seminary students at the Lutheran Seminary. At the time it seemed appropriately ironic given my divorce from all things Lutheran. And by this time it was the 70's...an era arguably much harder to explain to those who didn't experience it...more difficult than the 60's perhaps.

Back then it seemed like everyone smoked pot...bankers, college students, cops...even so called "straight people". It felt as if we were trying to get the angst (and it was mostly angst) of the 1960's behind us by throwing caution to the wind and experimenting. The so-called "Establishment" couldn't be trusted to tell the truth after all the lies of the previous decade. And grass was *cheap*! Fifteen bucks could purchase a four-finger bag (the depth of the herb in the baggie) of "Mexican" pot that would get you high enough to feel somewhat euphoric and giggly...unlike today's pot which can leave you sitting on the couch drooling on yourself wondering why Radiohead goes so well with NFL football. Or so I have read in a magazine. Thus began my "making up for lost time" era.

Whether I smoked an exorbitant amount of marijuana is open for debate. Those who frown on it would say a lot. Stoners might have called me an amateur. I'm not here to lecture anyone or make a value judgment. A little experimentation without being overtly reckless is probably a good thing in my mind. I did give it up for good finally. I had a *very good reason* to quit...give it up entirely...although it uh...hmm...escapes me at the moment. Funny, I can vividly recall the *first* time I smoked it but cannot for the life of me remember the *last*. But...it don't matter *MAN!!* (Before there was "dude"...there was "man".)

So one day I just finish smoking a doobie of this Mexican and my wife Yvonne says to me, "I'm going shopping at Gold Circle. Wanna come along?" For those of you too young to remember, Gold Circle was a decent discount store that later became what is now Kohl's. A single story store with clothing, household items, etc. Not particularly interesting. But when you're stoned just about anything mundane can seem interesting...sometimes exciting even. I said "sure".

It being a warm late spring day I was in a t-shirt and cutoff shorts and Yvonne wore cutoffs as well with a bright yellow tube top. A tube top was a stretchy piece of material that was worn over the breasts not unlike a rubber band around some items you were trying to keep together. It was worn sans bra. No self-respecting woman in 1977 wore a bra. At the time she had her blond hair very, long and straight...almost waist length. It was her neo-hippie "make up for lost time" phase as well. Although her parents might just say I was a bad influence on her...still might. I don't care. She looked mighty fine to me.

We're meandering around the store when I wander off to look at something across the way...doesn't matter *what* because I probably forgot 5 minutes after I looked at it anyway. Then I see the long blond hair, the bright yellow tube top and frayed cutoffs and begin following at a safe husbandly distance. Five...maybe ten minutes pass...it's hard to tell when you're high...and I'm getting a little anxious to go home and drink a cup of hot coffee while eating a bowl of ice cream. Still she continues looking at frocks and such hanging on a rack instead of sensing my cravings! This makes me more and more frustrated. I *must* experience the sensual extreme polarities of hot and cold soon! Can't she realize that? What's *wrong* with her anyway? This is when I get into the stereotypical husband mood of shortness at which I excel!!

Finally I grab an elbow, whirl her around, look her directly in the eyes and say, "Are you gonna BUY something or are you gonna *fuck around ALL DAY?!*"

The usual annoyed wifely "whatever" look I should have gotten was replaced by one of shock mixed with a bit of bemusement.

It was NOT Yvonne! It was a different woman with long blond hair, frayed cutoffs and bright yellow tube top!! My face flushed red like a tomato and the sounds coming out of my mouth were only amping up my turmoil.

"UHHHH…BWAA!!! BLAH Sorry!! Bwaph – uh – duh duh!!

My brain failed me as well. I could not for the life of me get it engaged. And I knew saying "My, you certainly look great in that bright yellow tube top" was NOT going to help matters. After what seemed like my 50th attempt at "Sorry." I began a manic search for the woman I came in with.

Once I found Yvonne I was no better at explaining

to her why we needed to leave Gold Circle…hell…the STATE…as soon as possible.

"Whatsamatter?"

"BWAH! DUH-DAH! UHHHHH…Hubbubububub."

I told Yvonne my story later over a cup of hot coffee and a bowl of ice cream.

Frank Sinatra once sang, "Regrets…I have a few…but too few to mention." But I have one regret I'm willing to share with you now.

I regret tube tops ever went out of style.

Broken Key

I hadn't realized I did it until I got in the car and tried putting the key in the ignition. It didn't go in smoothly. Taking a look at the key I saw it was broken...pretty much right in half. Stuff like this starts happening when your car is almost 20 years old. A '91 Miata...silver. And dirty. I hardly ever wash the thing. I like to fancy myself the detective Paul Newman played in that old 60's flick *Harper.* Except he drove an old Porsche. And I think it was primer gray. Okay...so it's not the same thing. It's close enough for me.

My Miata was already scheduled for a front brake job so I figured the dealer could fish the key out while it was there. The guy on the phone said if they couldn't it was $400 for a new ignition. Wow. When I dropped it off a sign behind the desk read:

LABOR - $80 per HOUR

Wow again. I hoped for the best.

The next day at work I got the call. No dice on the broken key. But the manager told me a locksmith could probably get it out for a lot less than a new ignition. No shit. I've bought entire vehicles for less than $400.

But I procrastinated...as usual...since I could start the car with a broken key. And every time I did I thought, "Man...somebody could steal this car pretty easy!" Something new on my worry list. Even after I found a place that would fix it...it'd take "just a few minutes", she said on the phone...I waited. On a putty gray Friday afternoon I knocked off work early and drove to the locksmith.

The place was in a rough neighborhood. An area where good people who deserve better still, live because they can't afford any place else...and it's their home. The business had a sign that must have hung there since the Great Depression. There were bars on the windows and a notice that read "Guard Dog On Duty". A dog works here...that's what I thought. I ambled in where there was a small waiting area. Most of the room was behind a counter with what had to be thousands of keys on the walls. In and on the counter were key fobs, rings, chains...anything that might have something to do with locks.

I waited behind a stooped over, old black man. Waiting on him behind the counter was a middle aged, Appalachian woman...pale white with bleached blonde hair, wearing a sweatshirt and blue jeans. Rugged yet somehow feminine. "Now all's ya gotta do

Hon is get them pins oughta that lock, bring 'em in here and we'll fix ya right up! No need ta buy no new lock!" she was telling the old man. He thanked her, turned, smiled at me and went out the door.

"What can I do for ya?" she asked me.

"I broke my car key off..."

"You the guy who called a few days ago?" she asked sweetly with a swagger that made it sound like, "Where the hell you been?"

"That's me."

"Car out front?"

"It's next to the building."

"I'll meet ya there." She said grabbing some small tools and a can of WD40.

As I passed through the front door I heard her yell, "Frank! The dog's made a mess!" I whipped around and saw a huge, black dog...seemingly friendly...at least while he was "off the clock". This wasn't just his job. It was his home.

The woman was already standing next to the Miata. The color of her bleached hair seemed all the more...um...bleached...like a piece of the sun against the gray afternoon. "This is one tiny car, Hon" she quipped. I let her in. She immediately utilized the WD40 and went to work with tiny tools the likes of which I'd never seen. After about 3 or 4 minutes I started to think she'd never get that piece of key out of there and I'd have to spend maybe $800 or more at the dealership. Suddenly she turned to me, smiled a pretty smile and chirped, "Almost got it!" Two minutes later we were heading back into the shop...me through the front door...her in the side.

"That was amazing." I said at the counter.

Looking slightly embarrassed...sheepishly emboldened...she replied, "Yep! Sometimes it pays to know how to break into things!"

I...had no comment.

"That's 5 bucks. You need a spare Hon?"

"Yeah...uh...yeah" I stammered, knowing full well I already had all the keys I needed.

Flying V

It started as early as grade school I suppose. Whenever some obnoxious kid in my class chanted "Ricky and Susie sittin' in a tree. K I S S I N G! First comes love. Then comes marriage. Then comes a baby in the baby carriage!!!" And unlike most children my age...it wasn't really the kissing part that I objected to. Not even the marriage thing. It was the *baby.* I cringed at the word and thought something like "Shouldn't we enjoy ourselves a little first?"

I'm sure the fact that I was the oldest of four in a working class family, struggling to make ends meet, didn't endear me to children. I had to help take care of my siblings who always seemed to get whatever I had to wait for...at the very same time I was allowed. The four summers as a camp counselor with groups of 13 year old boys didn't help either.

Then there was the time in college...I was helping take inner city kids out trick or treating. I had gotten friendly with a woman who was in the group that night, so we were hanging together watching our respective one night foster kids beg for candy. I found her attractive and interesting and sensed she felt the same for me. Except right when I was seriously thinking of asking her out...I had to give some adult like instructions to my beggar child. She turned to me and cooed, "You will make a very good father some day!" I immediately lost interest in her.

I don't by any means hate children. I think babies are cute and wonderful and all that. The people acting goofy around them bothers me more than a baby crying does. Now the "after they are a baby part"...*that* gives me the heebie jeebies. And I do feel that just about every experience in life is better without children involved. Call me Scrooge. I don't care.

So when I started dating my wife Yvonne...when it was getting serious...we talked about having kids. But we mostly talked about *not having kids*. Of course most of our friends would say, "Oh you'll change your minds!!! Wait and see!!" I waited until I was 35. That was long enough. Yvonne and I again talked it over and decided...I volunteered...to get a vasectomy.

I found a doctor...his name escapes me now. You'll understand why it does later. And I went in for the interview type appointment where he asked me questions I knew he would ask like, "Do you think...even remotely...that you might change your mind?" And, "What if you get married again later in life and your new wife wants a child?" I was ready for *those* questions. It was when he asked me if I had a girlfriend that I got puzzled. I mean...if I DID have a girlfriend...and I didn't want to get my WIFE pregnant...wouldn't it stand to reason I wouldn't want to get my GIRLFRIEND pregnant?" Still...I kept my smart-ass thoughts to myself and said "no".

So I went in for the "procedure". The nurse put me in one of those backless gowns and I immediately thought, "Hey!!! The stuff's up in FRONT!!" I was then unceremoniously strapped to an operating table and given a shot of Novocain in my scrotum. (Not to worry...I will cease using polite medical terms as the story unfolds!!) It's what the doctor called "a local". I'd call it "localized torture" because hey...I'm laying there strapped on a table and he's getting the syringe ready...which seems to take like a day and a half...and of course there is not ONE shot...but one shot for EACH SIDE of my uh...scrotum.

I tried to look at the clock while listening to the snipping sounds, while the doctor and nurse had a mundane conversation concerning what they had watched on TV the night before. At one point I winced so I was given yet ANOTHER shot. You know...just so I wouldn't *feel anything*. As daunting as the scene was, I tried to remind myself the "procedure" would be much shorter than say...the lifespan of offspring. I felt like a car getting tuned up...watching myself being operated on.

As I lay there watching this doctor begin to stitch up my...uh...scrotum...he began telling me about the healing process and that I would be required to come in periodically and give a sample until he could...in his best judgment...tell me that "the little guys aren't a swimming no more!!" So I did...diligently. Every month I would go back to his office where they would give me a girlie magazine and a cup and put me in a private room so that I could...uh...make a contribution. It was about the third time...the third month of contributing that I began wondering about things. First off...these people were not the best in replenishing their porn library. I mean...anybody who knows ANYTHING about porn realizes that you get *used to it* and have to buy some *new porn*. That's why it's such a lucrative endeavor...at least that's one reason.

At four months I almost asked an attractive young nurse if she could come in the room with me and uh...lend a hand...or two. But I was polite and refrained. Yet once in the room I realized it was yes...the *same fucking girlie magazines* I'd been uh...looking at...for the past 4 months!! I felt like opening the door and shouting, "Doesn't anybody out there have a *fucking movie?*!!!" I mean...literally.

Five months after the "procedure" I again...dutifully...contributed as much to the cup as I could given the fact that yes...they still had not purchased new stimuli. But afterwards...rather than being sent home...I was called into the doctor's office. He had me take a seat. He looked at me solemnly and shook his head back and forth.

"I do NOT understand it!!" Doc muttered. I've been doing these procedures for years now...over 3000 of them."

I asked him what he was getting at...knowing full well what was on his mind.

"The little guys...they are STILL swimming around."

I asked him how that could be. I offered the theory that somehow...miraculously...a vas defers had reattached itself and was back in business.

"Highly improbable" was his response. "Some men...very few mind you...have a third vas defers...usually behind the testicles (that's what's in the uh...scrotum by the way)"

Then he looked directly at me and said, "I'd like to try again."

I felt queasy and said, "You want to do it *again*?"

The doctor nodded earnestly.

"You're going to take my BALLS out aren't you?" I replied.

Incredulously his response was a matter of fact "only temporarily."

My mind immediately raced back to an old high school joke. A guy is getting his family jewels operated on (reason unclear) and his balls fall out and roll out of the room. The nurse says, "DOCTOR!!! The patient's balls just rolled out of the room! Should I go get them?" The doctor yells, "There's no time for that!!! Get my lunch over there in the corner and give me the two onions I packed!!!" So the nurse does as she is told and the doctor sews onions in the guy's...uh...scrotum.

A few weeks later the guy comes in for a follow up and the doctor asks him how he's feeling. The guy says "I feel great except for one really weird thing". The doctor asks him what this weird thing is and the guys says, "Every time I walk by a McDonald's I get a *hard on*!!"

Ba rum pum pum!!

This is honestly the first thing that popped into my mind. Shortly after that, "no way in living hell" took its place.

One percent. That's how many vasectomies fail. 99

percent do not. My luck at the lotto should have these odds. Anyway...that's my sordid unlikely tale. After all the money this doctor made on my failed "procedure" there was no way I would go through it again.

Besides. I'd already seen every magazine this doctor owned...and I haven't been by a McDonalds in years.

Qube

It was the mid 1970's...1977 to be exact...when what was then simply Warner Cable initiated an interactive cable system in Columbus, Ohio. It was called...for some unknown reason...Qube. Being the first cable network in this city...and this was back when cable monopolies were legal...if you had cable you had Qube.

Maybe it was called Qube after the box that sat on your living room's coffee table. I'm not referring to the cable box underneath the television. This was a very large remote control. Back then...in the dark ages...you actually had to GET UP and turn the DIAL to change channels. No kidding kids. So this was the very first remote control most of us ever had. Just set your television's dial to 03 and you never had to get up to change channels again. Qube had buttons all over it, was about 8 inches by 12 inches and maybe 2 inches thick. You couldn't misplace this "remote" if you wanted to. Besides being huge it had what looked like the Trans-Atlantic Cable running from it, across your living room floor, and into the box under your T.V. Most Qube subscribers tripped over this garden hose sized cable on a daily basis...including me.

But…AAAAHHH…the simple joys of those heady days of virgin cable television! For the first time in a man's life he had porn right there in his house…without having to go somewhere and purchase it!! I mean…sure…it was mostly a lot of "head bobbing" shots. But there were bare, bouncing breasts galore!!! And…there were devious schemes to get this head bobbin' bare breasted fare for free. Men…skulking in dark corners could be overheard whispering, "Did you hear that if you put a stack of magnets over number 20 you can get porn for free?" Or, "It's true!! All you have to do is jam a large safety pin in the Qube box right by the 'send' button and you won't get billed for porn!!"

Sometimes I really miss the 70's…even though I did get busted for the safety pin idea. I was watching something akin to "Head Bobbin' Beach Babes Bare Their Bouncing Breasts in Biloxi" when the picture scrambled. Every frikkin' channel was scrambled. I panicked and began pushing the big safety pin into the Qube like a possessed Voodoo Doctor!! When the repair guy confronted me about it I stammered, "Uh…I think somebody messed with it at a party I had." He shook his head in disgust and muttered, "Sure…sure." He'd heard about the giant safety pin theory…no doubt.

What made Qube different from other city's cable

systems was that it was interactive. That is, you could send responses back to the television studio by casting "votes" on the Qube remote box. A range of numbers from 1 to 4…I think…and there were "yes" and "no" buttons…at the bottom of the thing that let you communicate with the broadcaster. There were shows where you could "vote" for you favorite video…how the chef on the cooking show should make "your" eggs…weird concepts like that. The one show that caught my eye was their daily talent show. This was when I was just starting to play in Columbus as a musician.

I can't remember the name of the talent show. It was on Monday through Friday in the late afternoon. The first four days would showcase 3 or 4 acts that would perform and at the end viewers at home would vote for the winner. The four daily winners would then return Friday for the weekly championship. And, of course there were monthly winners and finally a grand prizewinner for the year. Prizes were donated by local businesses and could be anything from a haircut to a massage to a dinner for two at a local eatery. I decided to give it a shot.

I took my guitar and harmonica down to Warner Qube studios and auditioned. I played a mean version of Bob Dylan's "All Along the Watchtower" with a wicked harmonica solo. I passed the audition. Of course no one ever *failed* an audition. I guess it was just a formality to give the director the choice of a variety of acts on specific shows. I was told to come back next Tuesday for the competition.

The days leading up to Tuesday were filled with anxiety...practice...fret...practice. You get the idea. The day finally arrived and as I sat waiting my turn I was surprised to see a live audience. I'd *heard* them on television but was never sure if they were real or amateurishly recorded. But there they were sitting in small bleachers off to the side of the stage...people from all walks of life...children...teenagers...retired folks. People who had nothing better to do at 5 o'clock in the afternoon. I reassured myself by assuming the ones voting for the winner were all those sophisticated viewers at home...the educated, middle class who could afford Qube in their homes. Sure.

I played. I kicked ass. I won. There I stood at the end of the show...in front of the camera...next to the smiling, camera waving hosts, clutching my little plastic trophy...credits rolling...applause filling the room. "And I'm sure you'll want to come back on Friday to compete in the weekly final won't you Rick?" the beautiful woman co-host was chirping to me. "Uh huh." fell out of my open mouth. This seemed the most exciting thing to happen to me since my instrumental surf band...the Illusions...won the junior high talent show when I was in the 7th grade. My career as a singer/songwriter was well on its way!!!

The next couple days I was floating...savoring the exuberance of my sweet victory. My father and mother took Friday afternoon off work so most of my family could be at Qube Studios for the Friday weekly final. I was confident. And although I didn't know exactly who the other contestants were, I had watched the show enough times to know I had a very good chance of at least winning one more time. Besides, all my friends would be watching and many of them would be pushing the button on their Qube boxes...votes for *me* magically streaming through the thick cable, accumulating at the studio culminating in yet another triumph for the guy with the Guild D-50 guitar.

Friday came. My wife...my mom and dad...my sister...they were all sitting in the bleachers on the Qube talent show set. I reprised the torrid rendition of "All Along the Watchtower" one more time. The audience loved it...especially the harmonica part at the end. My family beamed at me. I felt good.

But then the karma shifted. An older gentleman...a 75-year-old guy...nice guy I found out later...came out with a handsaw and a violin bow. Now this was hardly the first time I'd seen someone play the saw. There was a peculiar teacher from my high school who taught typing...he played the saw every year in the high school talent show. Mr. Mossman...weird guy. Good saw player...I think. If you've never had the pleasure of listening to someone play a Sears Craftsman handsaw...well...the word that comes to mind is "unearthly". It's a kind of almost continuous whining...like lost souls calling to heaven for rescue...for the promise of eternal sleep. And as this old man drew his bow over the bent saw blade I could see the somewhat uneasy inquisitiveness of the faces of the studio audience. When he finished they applauded politely. I felt confused.

When the final votes came in it was close. But the 75-year-old man with the handsaw was declared the weekly winner. I finished second...to a man and his handsaw. I was beside myself with dismay. I was in shock. My family tried to cheer me up. "Make the best of it son...it's just a bunch of kids at home voting on their parents' cable." my father reassured me. But I tried to make sense out of it. And the lesson I eventually learned is that many times the only sense of things in this life is *nonsense*...and that's not always a bad thing. And the nonsense continued with the two of us up on stage at the end of the weekly finals. The bubbling hosts...while the credits rolled and the audience applauded...handed out our prizes. Me...I got a jar of Orville Redenbacher Popcorn. The 75-year-old guy...he got a pair of bright red Speedos.

Somehow this made me feel better.

So if you're at the beach someday...and you see a 105 year old man romping around in a bright red Speedo...walk up and congratulate him. But you may have to wind your way through a throng of bare breasted bouncing beach babes swooning to the eerie, hypnotic sound of him playing...oh so earnestly...a Sears Craftsman handsaw.

Hope "Big Ass Springs" Eternal

On the day I was born...during childbirth...the doctors discovered that my mother's tailbone was broken. I don't know the extent of the injury but I'm assuming it was cracked because, if I remember the story correctly, she had ridden the roller coaster a few months earlier at Puritas Springs...a long forgotten amusement park close to where I spent my childhood. While I'm to this day uncertain of the validity of this tale (just like the rumors that as many as three people had perished riding this particular coaster) I suppose it WOULD explain a lot of things if it is...in fact...true. On top of this I was a breech baby...feet first. Apparently I had a hunch as to how cold and cruel this cold and cruel world actually is.

So I'm in the middle of all this...feet sticking out of the womb...struggling to stay inside despite the cracked vertebrae...and science being what it was in those days...the days before c-sections...the doctors used forceps to help get me out. Why...I couldn't say...but that's what they used.
Forceps...sheesh...double sheesh. And they poked me right in the friggin' left eye with those pointy forceps!

Before I'm even smacked on the ass I'm legally blinded in one eye with sharp...pointy...forceps!! This day...my very FIRST day...was not going well. So they yanked the rest of me out, slapped my itty, bitty butt and everything...with the exception of my left eye...is okay. Now if this had happened in 1991 instead of 1951 I'd have lived in the lap of luxury as a child because of the big out of court settlement. But back then I suppose the doctors convinced my parents that I was lucky to get off that easy. So I grew up lucky...and poor.

In the days following the very first, I became overly sensitive to that classic gem of parental wisdom almost every mom and dad whip out at any given time when they don't like what you're doing. Admittedly, the phrase is good because it can be used in so many situations. Like..."HEY! Drop that stick! You wanna put somebody's eye out with that thing?" Or..."Don't run with the scissors! You wanna put your eye out or something?" (a little aside...I don't think I've ever met anyone who actually WANTED to put their eye out...or something. But I do remember seeing a movie when I was in high school called "Hawaii". There's this scene where...for some reason I forget...this guy thrusts a big stick INTO his eye and upon seeing this I thought, "Holy Shit!! That guy put his eye out on PURPOSE!!!" I made a mental note of the fact that he wasn't even running.) But I would think strange thoughts whenever I'd hear this phrase being used...still do actually. If it's directed towards someone beside myself I might think something like, "Go ahead and PUT your eye out buddy! Then you'll know how I feel!" Or perhaps, "Yep...put your eye out. Then when you play baseball you'll strike out as much as I did in Little League!"...which I'm not sure is mathematically possible. If my Mom and Dad said something to me like "Ricky! Don't shoot that arrow straight up in the air! It's liable to come down and put your eye out!" I would think to myself, "Geez...I hope it puts my LEFT eye out. It's pretty fucking bogus as it is."

A couple of summers ago my wife and I had this nice new deck and patio put in our backyard. If you've been to our house you'll remember we've ALWAYS had trouble with the gate coming into the yard. First we had this rickety picket fence where you had to literally pick up the gate to move it because it was sagging so much. Then...my friend Dan (the man behind the curtain) and I built a new fence and gate...which was fine for about three months until the dirt settled...and the gate warped...and the latch got out of whack and wouldn't hold the gate shut anymore. So for like...seven years...we used a bungee cord to keep it shut...which if you were carrying groceries in from the car or something, the aforementioned cord of bungee would invariably fly somewhere far away when you unhooked it. So we kept a supply of bungee cords on the back porch near the gate...for like...seven years. Unfortunately, the guy who built the new deck and patio AND brand new gate built a gate that only latched from inside the yard. I told him at the time this wasn't going to work because you had to be able to get INTO the patio. I guess I saw no point in spending lots of money on a patio you couldn't get into because the gate was latched. So to correct his oversight he put this BIG ASS spring on it so it would swing shut and there would be no need to latch it. And it worked fine...for a while.

A few days after the project was completed I was coming in from the garage and stopped to listen to one of the guy next door's God awful salesperson type jokes when Henri (my pooch) heard us and started going CRAZY!! Pretty soon he burst through the gate like a thoroughbred starting the Kentucky Derby! I found this dismaying because the tension on the BIG ASS spring was already strong enough to crack walnuts. But I decided I better make it tighter. So...I'm out there tightening and tightening when all of a sudden...PHHWWAAAMM!! The fucking spring FLEW into pieces everywhere. Some have yet to be found. This pissed me off big time. I ended up at the Andersons buying a latch I HOPED would work...and another BIG ASS spring...just to be sure. (another little aside...I find it somewhat disconcerting that on this day I purchased not just gate hardware but a couple bottles of nice French wine, a T.V. tray and some charcoal...all under the same roof. This is something I cannot get used to.) Pretty soon I was back by the gate in 95 degrees weather with a heat index of what had to be 9000 trying to get this new latch to fit the gate from hell...which it never did. This was about the time I began to think my yard was the goddamned Bermuda Triangle for gates. After much frustration I moved to "Plan B"...put on another BIG ASS spring...not too original I suppose...but in the heat it was all I could come up with. I got the damned thing on with no problems. I followed the directions meticulously. It looked good and I was feeling pretty proud of myself because most of the time after one of my home improvement projects we have to take out a home equity loan to have things fixed correctly. Now came time for the initial GRAND OPENING of the brand new gate with the brand new BIG ASS spring Rick put on all by himself!!! So...I began to push the gate open...ever so slowly when...PHHHWWWAAAMMM!!!... the fucking thing FLEW apart in pieces all over the place...some of which have yet to be found. This...once again...pissed me off big time.

To make an already too long story short...I got a little wimpy assed screen door spring that shuts the gate from hell just fine thank you. I have to keep an eye on Henri...but that's okay. While I was installing this little wimpy assed screen door spring it dawned on

me...I could have put my EYE out (or something) with that BIG ASS spring!!! It also occurred to me that...if this HAD happened...that I put my eye out I mean...I would definitely prefer my left eye. That thing's already pretty fucking bogus as it is.

Strange Carma

We bought it in 1991...brand new. A Mazda Miata.
The model was introduced in 1989 and my wife
Yvonne and I finally got sick and tired of
pushing...towing...repairing the two early 70's MGBs
we owned. I reassured our mechanic we'd have him
work on our new Miata. He laughed and replied, "You
guys buy a Miata and I'll never see you again!" I *did*
see him again...ran into him at a Joan Baez concert a
couple years ago. Somehow I don't think that's what
he was talking about.

Yvonne insisted on silver. I wasn't about to argue.
After all, this is as much a toy as it is an automobile.
And that's what we bought...silver with black
interior. At first we took turns driving our cute little
roadster. One week I drove it. The next it was her
turn...which was okay except it's one of those cars
where, when adjusting the seat to fit the length of
your legs you keep wishing there was a spot right IN
BETWEEN the two that aren't quite right.
No...wait...too close...no wait...a little too far...now
too close...now too far. This "every other Monday

adjusting the seat" ritual may be why...even though the car is in *her* name...for all intents and purposes...it became *my* car. Yvonne more than likely has a way different story concerning this. But I'm the one writing this...so take my word for it.

I've babied my Miata. It's been garaged almost every day of its life. Okay...so I don't wash it very often. The thing's like 3 inches off the ground!!! Washing and drying off a car that low to the ground on a regular basis? Hell...I'd be in traction by now...might even be using a walker!!! If you think I'm kidding watch me get out of it sometime.

Soon after buying our car I began to think it was jinxed. Within the first four months I had been hit TWICE. And not by just anybody either but by two UNINSURED motorists! How's *that* for luck? The second accident was the worst. I was sideswiped by a drunken crack head chick, that left the scene when I went to call the cops. And the saddest part of the whole thing was she had a baby with her...a tiny baby in a baby carrier. After the police arrived and I described her...well...they knew exactly who I was talking about. "Oh yeah, she lives with her ex-con boyfriend around here somewhere." Great...just great. To make a long sordid tale short, the first guy who hit me at least got his wages garnisheed. The crack head chick and her ex-con boyfriend skipped town.

Fortunately for me, Yvonne and the Miata...my luck changed immediately. I have yet to be in another wreck. Nineteen years without a mishap involving another driver be they insured or not. So when I had the car washed and detailed early this past summer and noticed a small spot of rust by the driver's side door, I thought, "*surface rust*". Why wouldn't I? Garaged every day...zero accidents...no dents...the car has been the most dependable thing I've ever driven. With this optimism I took it to a reputable body shop for an estimate. I'm thinking...800 bucks...maybe a thousand.

A young guy came out and introduced himself as Rob. I told Rob about the *surface rust* by the driver's door. He shook his head.

"I hope you're right sir. But you know...rust can be a *cancer*."

"*Cancer*?" I replied...thinking he was being overly melodramatic.

"Yeah. *Cancer.* Your car might LOOK clean. But underneath...where you can't see...well...it can be like *cancer*" he intoned as he helped visualize by moving his hands over the car's surface.

Wow. My mind raced back to an old Neil Young album, "Rust Never Sleeps". His title came from a marketing campaign. Some of the guys who later formed Devo had worked for a marketing company and that's the slogan they came up with for a body shop. But that seemed friendly compared with, "Hey buddy. Sit down. I gotta tell ya something. I'm afraid your car...has...*cancer*. Pretty far along too I'm afraid." And ya know what? That ended up being Rob's diagnosis.

"Mr. Brown."

"Yes, Rob?"

"It's *cancer*. Spread up here in the front quarter panel...not to mention some of the back quarter panel. Bad."

When he brought out the written estimate it was more than twice the figure I'd imagined. Life is like that...more often than not. Yvonne and I talked it over...thought about how nice it is without a car payment...and decided to have Surgeon Rob take care of our baby.

I called and we set a date.

"How long will it be before she's done?" I inquired before saying goodbye to my ride.

"Can't be sure...until we get in there. Don't know how bad it is yet." Rob said solemnly.

I thought, "Wow...*cancer*."

About a week goes by and both of us naively think maybe our Miata is almost finished...the paint is drying right now. Then I get a call at work…from Rob.

"Mr. Brown?"

"Yes?"

"You need to come out here and…well…we took both fenders off and…well…you really should come out here and look for yourself."

So I did. I drove out to look at my sick automobile. But while backing out of a parking spot in the garage I clobbered the driver's side mirror on our Jeep Cherokee. Omen # 1. I popped it back into place and drove off to the "car hospital."

The receptionist called for Rob.

"Mr. Brown is here to see you."

Rob met me in the lobby and took me back to my car. It was in pieces spread out in a circle maybe 15 feet in diameter. He pointed to the quarter panels. But that's not what shocked me. Below…on the floor…on either side of the car…right beneath where the quarter panels had been removed…was a pile of rust…a pile that seemed to be 6 inches tall. *Cancer.*

"I though you should see it for yourself. And I'm afraid we're going to have to burn out the rocker panels and replace them as well."

"Uh…yeah. Thanks Rob." *Cancer.*

So a day later I'm faxed yet another estimate. This time it's more than THREE times what I had originally thought the total would be. Yeah…I know...life is like that...but does it ALWAYS have to be like that? And in the meantime I'm going out to yet another car place to have the Cherokee's mirror replaced...sigh.

Two days short of a month. That's how long the Miata has been in the shop when Rob calls and tells me it's finished. Great! Hallelujah!! It's late August so there will be plenty of convertible time left in the year. (You do not drive a Miata in the snow. It goes nowhere.) And now maybe I'll quit having that reoccurring nightmare where someone...uninsured probably...smashes into my newly repaired Miata! Yvonne and I are both excited about getting the roadster back. She's been driving a loaner from her workplace. And that was fortunate. On the downside...the car is a 1994 Chrysler New Yorker that is affectionately named the "pimpwagon". I have yet to hear Yvonne wistfully reminisce about her adventures in the "pimpwagon."

So on a drizzling Saturday morning the two of us drive out to meet Rob and bring our baby home.

"Look! There it is!!1 Out front!! It looks GREAT!!" I exclaim.

"They put it right out front...like they're proud of it!" Yvonne adds.

And as we stroll towards our shining 1991 Mazda Miata, I reach up to adjust the glasses on my face. And the lens pops out of the right side into my hand.

"Jeeeezzz!" I moan. Omen # 2.

Yvonne assures me she will tape my glasses together good enough to get me to the optometrist once we go into the office to pay. The fact that the car looked almost brand new lifted my spirits. So we went inside with Rob and Yvonne taped my eyewear back together while I pretended to see the bill and sign the Visa paperwork. We shake hands with Rob…tell him he did a nice job…and head toward our vehicles. I climb inside the Miata and notice the side view mirror to my left is out of whack. I reach over to adjust it…and…THE MIRROR BREAKS OFF IN MY LEFT HAND!!!!!!!!!!!!!!!!!!!!!!! I immediately think, *"Cancer!"*

I sauntered back into the body shop office tightly gripping the mirror in my hand.

"Whaddyathinkathis?" I ask the good car doctor. I don't think I've ever seen a man more embarrassed in my life. And I suppose he should have been. For the next few days…after getting my eyeglasses repaired…I drove a magnificent looking 1991 Mazda Miata with no left side mirror. And for a guy who's legally blind in his left eye that makes for quite an adventure. But I figure 2 car accidents and a broken mirror is a pretty good track record for a 14 year old car...a car that...at least for the time being...has beaten...*cancer.*

And I guess there's one other good thing that's come of this frustrating car story. That physical I've been putting off for a while now...I think I'll call and make an appointment.

Holiday Cheer from Aunt Edith

My late Uncle Wes lived with my Aunt Edith for most of his adult life...although I'm sure it seemed like an eternity to him. He worked for the Bethlehem Steel Company in Baltimore for thirty years until he retired. He worked the night shift getting off around 7 a.m. when he would come home for dinner. In the summer when it was warm...and Baltimore can get very, very humid...he would go to a movie matinee in an air conditioned theater and sleep. If you knew my Aunt Edith you would assume what I did...even as a child...and that was that Uncle Wes worked nights and went to matinees to get away from his wife. He never said much. He was a slight, wiry man of few words. And the few words he almost always uttered were, "For Chrissakes Edith! SHUDD UPP!!"

The man was almost incidental by nature. One time...after he retired and he and Aunt Edith moved back to the Cleveland area...my brothers and I were helping him put a refrigerator in a backyard shed because there was no room for it in the trailer they were moving into. After much jostling my brothers and I closed the shed door and thought we were finished. From her perch (as supervisor of course) Aunt Edith looked at the three of us with bewilderment and asked, "Where the HELL is Wes?" And after exchanging confused glances we heard muffled sounds coming from behind the fridge in the shed. "MMMPPPHH!!! Hey!! HHMMPPHHFFF!!!" We quickly opened the shed door, moved aside the refrigerator and liberated Uncle Wes. My brothers and I were all embarrassed and each, in turn, apologized profusely for our insensitive behavior. Aunt Edith broke into the humility with a shriek of, "What the HELL were you doing in there?" Which prompted Uncle Wes to...once again...chant his mantra. "For Chrissakes Edith!! SHUDD UPP!!" They were quite the loving couple. Their last name was Crabtree. I am not making this up.

Wes soon was diagnosed with lung cancer. Thirty years in the steel mills and 2 packs a day of Chesterfield non-filters caught up with him. The last time I saw him he was lying on the couch in their trailer smoking the aforementioned brand of cigarettes, quite literally coughing his lungs out...or what was left of them. "I TOLD him to quit those goddamned things years ago. " Aunt Edith offered for my contemplation. To which Uncle Wes replied sarcastically (yep, you guessed it) "Cough cough...For

Chrissakes HACK! HACK! Edith!!! SHUDD UPPP!!!"
These were the final words I heard my uncle ever say
and we all joked at the funeral that these very words
were more than likely chiseled into his headstone.

A few years after Wes passed, my brother and his
new wife were having their very first Christmas and
invited everyone over...including Aunt Edith. My
parents were there along with my siblings and their
families. This included my brother Jim's 9-year-old
stepson Matt. Matt the Brat was what my father
called him. I thought this surprisingly subtle for my
Dad. If I knew where Matt is today...and thank God I
do not...I would have to guess some one killed him or
he's in jail convicted of several murders. I honestly
don't care so long as he's nowhere near me. So Matt
the Brat is playing with one of the toys some one so
graciously gave him and he broke it. This kid could
break anything he got his hands on. But in a moment
of diplomacy my father (affectionately known as
Snook) said, "They don't make anything any good any
more!!" To which...in the spirit of the season Aunt
Edith quipped, "You're right Snook!! Everything IS
SHIT!!!" Well...happy holidays to you too Aunt Edith.
Inside my head I distinctly heard a voice from my
past reply, "For Chrissakes Edith!! SHUDD UPPP!"

You know...there are lots of reasons to go through
life believing that "everything is shit." There are days

when it certainly seems true to me. I have my days when Sartre's "Hell is other people" could easily be the thought of the day. But...unlike Aunt Edith...I don't want to spend a big chunk of my life living alone in a trailer. And when I think of this particular Christmas it strikes me how most of them blur into each other...with the exception of a few. And this is one of them I distinctly remember. As much as family...and sometimes even friends...can annoy a person...especially at this time of year...I have come to realize that even some one like Aunt Edith helped make me who I have become. I mean that in a positive way. Imagine...Aunt Edith's negativity was so over the top it MADE me consider the positive. I have no idea how she became so bitter. My father did shortly before he died also. Yet they both, particularly Snook, had a positive influence. They were there. Unlike today when some people are not.

This holiday season...regardless of which one you celebrate...take the time to savor those around you...even if they drive you nuts. They may not...for whatever reason...be there next year. And in some strange way, which will surprise you, their absence will make you miss them. I guarantee it. (a possible exception to this uplifting message might be Matt the Brat) And you might consider that next year YOU might not be here. So I suppose my holiday message may seem bittersweet to most...but that's how I see it. And if anyone feels the need to take issue with my views then I encourage you to speak up LOUDLY...'cause I've got one thing and one thing only to say to you.

FOR CHRISSAKES!!!!

SHUDD UPPP!!!

Editor's note: Aunt Edith died a few years ago. She was 90 years old. Her neighbor called my Uncle Bruce and told him she had passed out in her trailer. He went and got her up...asked if she was all right and she said she was. He suggested she go to the hospital to make sure everything was okay. She told him to go to hell and get out of her house. He did just that...returning an hour later and she was gone. Sad...surely. But she lived her last day the way she lived every previous one. And despite her surliness I will miss my Aunt Edith this Christmas. And I will remember the one long ago when she informed us "Everything is shit!" Rest in peace Aunt Edith. I can picture Jesus turning to her and proclaiming, "Truly, truly I say unto you...For Wes's sake Edith...SHUDD UPPP!!!!!!!!!!!!!!!"

What the Ficken?

I suppose it was the fifth grade...somewhere around then...that I first encountered the word "fuck". Like most blue-collar parents...and perhaps most parents in general...my father and mother swore on occasion. But no one in his or her generation dared use the "f-word" except in the context of war. Soldiers have always said, "fuck". They're entitled to. Hearing the word and knowing what it meant or having an inkling of its versatility was lost on me. But hey...that used to be called innocence.

The f – word is all over the place now. And to be honest there are times I get sick of it. Yet I certainly oppose censoring the word because there are some people in this world...and they are few and far between...who have a real talent for using "fuck" (and all it's variations) to make a point, enhance humor, or clear the air. I enjoy being around a person who has a knack with "fuck". I once worked at a log splitter company (another tale in itself) with a guy named Mark. Mark was from Flint, Michigan. And if you've *ever* spent any time in Flint you know first hand that anyone who lives there...ever lived there...has every right to say, "fuck" whenever they want. It's the severely depressed city that's been home to filmmaker Michael Moore, writer Ben Hamper, and 60's and 70's unappreciated power trio Grand Funk (Fuck?) Railroad.

Mark, who outside of his rough vocabulary, was the sweetest guy you could ever know. Once I heard him swear I realized no one could equal his talent for utilizing arguably the most versatile word in the English language...or any language for that matter. If he was angry with someone...or disgusted...whatever...then Mark called them a "fuckknuckle". This really cracked us up there at the screw type log splitter company!! It's so original the word isn't even listed in *The **F** Word,* by Jesse Scheidlower (1995 Random House), a 232-page book devoted exclusively to the word "fuck" and its derivatives. Nowhere appears "fuckknuckle" and believe me there are plenty listed I haven't encountered. (And I've been around the fucking block a few times!)

Unicorn Log Splitters was a small shop with three younger guys (of which I include myself), the owner, and an older, retired guy who supposedly was the accountant. His name was Mr. McClintoch. I never saw Mr. McClintoch do much of anything except talk about drinking and in our brief careers there all of us drank with him at one time or another. Mark wasn't impressed with the guy. He nicknamed him "Mr. McFucktoch". I had to be *real careful* when addressing the old guy. "McFucktoch" stuck in your brain. And it's easier to say than McClintoch too. Mark was so creative with the f – word I realized he was the King. The "Fuck" King if you will.

Then there's Claus. He's the husband of a very good German friend of mine. My wife, Yvonne, and I have visited him and his better half Heike a few times. The very first trip we took to Europe we went to Altbach, Germany and stayed with them. Claus kind of reminded me of a German Mark in a lot of ways. Even though Claus is in his 40's he still loves heavy metal music...and I mean he LOVES it and loves it LOUD!! So did Mark. Claus may or may not swear like Mark. I can't tell. My German is horrible. Non-existent really. But they both certainly share the same bravado.

As a gesture of our gratitude for hosting us, Yvonne and I planned to take Claus and Heike out to a nice restaurant on our last night in Europe. After I made myself ready I went into the living room to try to have some sort of combination conversation/pantomime with Claus over the din of heavy metal, It was then I noticed his t – shirt. The front looked something like this:

fuck fuck fuck fuck fuck fuck fuck fuck fuck fuck fuck
fuck fuck fuck fuck fuck fuck fuck fuck fuck fuck fuck
fuck fuck fuck fuck fuck fuck fuck fuck fuck fuck fuck
fuck fuck fuck fuck fuck fuck fuck fuck fuck fuck fuck
fuck fuck fuck fuck fuck fuck fuck fuck fuck fuck fuck
fuck fuck fuck fuck fuck fuck fuck fuck fuck fuck fuck
fuck fuck fuck fuck fuck fuck fuck fuck fuck fuck fuck
fuck fuck fuck fuck fuck fuck fuck fuck fuck fuck fuck
fuck fuck fuck fuck fuck fuck fuck fuck fuck fuck fuck
fuck fuck fuck fuck fuck fuck fuck fuck fuck fuck fuck
fuck fuck fuck fuck fuck fuck fuck fuck fuck fuck fuck
fuck fuck fuck fuck fuck fuck fuck fuck fuck fuck fuck
fuck fuck fuck fuck fuck fuck fuck fuck fuck fuck fuck
fuck fuck fuck fuck fuck fuck fuck fuck fuck fuck fuck
fuck fuck fuck fuck fuck fuck fuck fuck fuck fuck fuck
fuck fuck fuck fuck fuck fuck fuck fuck fuck fuck fuck
fuck fuck fuck fuck fuck fuck fuck fuck fuck fuck fuck

I said, "Uh, Claus. Are you sure you want to wear
that shirt to dinner?" He had no idea what I was
getting at. "It says 'fuck' all over your shirt. Won't that
bother people?" I made my point to him. (His English
isn't much but he's a translator compared with me.)
Claus assured me that the American word "fuck" is
used all the time...in fun mostly. It didn't have the
same vulgarity in Germany because it's a foreign
term. "Ficken", Claus explained to me, "You don't

want to say *that!*" Okay. Fuck good...fun even.
Ficken...bad...except possibly in the United States.

A few months later...when it came time to buy
Claus a Christmas gift I knew exactly what to get
him...a Dead Kennedys "Too Drunk Too Fuck" t –
shirt. I figured if anyone in Germany was familiar
with these punkers and their underground "hit" it
would be Claus. I packaged it up and sent it off with
Heike's gift.

Shortly after Christmas I gave Heike a call to make
sure they received their holiday package and see how
they liked their presents. Heike answered so I chatted
with her a little while. Before I even got the chance to
ask about Claus I heard her tell him in German that
she was "speaking with Rick". Okay, I understood
"Rick" but I understood what was happening.
Immediately...over the heavy metal music of course, I
heard Claus shout joyously...in a way only he can do,
"TOO DRUNK TO FUCK!!!! TOO DRUNK TOO FUCK!!!
TOO DRUNK TO FUCK!!!"

"I guess Claus likes the shirt", I said.

"Oh sure, sure. You should not be surprised." Heike
replied.

"I couldn't find him one that read ficken" I joked
back.

Heike laughed her wonderful German laugh and

somehow I felt like we both knew...without saying...that Claus was something else...something else indeed. But there *is* one thing I do know for sure. That Claus...he ain't no fuckknuckle!!

The Autumn Outdoor Non – Fiction Theater of the

Truly Mundane

proudly presents:

Barbeque – The Return of Smokey Brown

Scene – early fall in the fenced in backyard of Smokey Brown. It is dusk and the sun is nearly set in the west. The fence is 5 feet tall on three sides facing the audience. Stage right has a vegetable garden. There is a gate in the fence stage left. Center stage is a Weber setting at the far end of a small patio situated immediately in front of the audience.

Smokey enters from the center of the audience as if coming out of his house from behind. He proceeds to crumple newspaper and put a ball of each underneath two charcoal chimney starters. He then places both into the bottom of the grill kettle. He fills each with gourmet wood charcoal. It is the bottom of the bag and as he empties it soot tops off the last chimney starter.

Smokey blows the excess soot from the tabletop, takes two or three long fireplaces matches and lights the newspapers beneath each chimney. He then strolls back into "the house" immediately behind the audience. Flames and smoke. (mostly smoke) pour out of the chimneys, increasing in intensity for about 5 minutes. Smoke wafts slowly over the fence stage left, hanging heavily in the early autumn darkness like a blanket of fog.

Smokey wanders back to center stage and examines the scene. By this time flames 18 inches high are licking out of the chimneys casting a campfire effect on the yard and patio.

Smokey hears a voice call out from behind the fence stage left.

"FIRE DEPARTMENT!!!"

Smokey first looks puzzled, and then glances at his next-door neighbor's deck and smiles.

Again, this time louder and much more forcefully,

"FIRE DEPARTMENT!!!"

Smokey cautiously edges his way towards the fence (stage left) when a firefighter's head pops over the

top of the fence. He/she shines a flashlight onto the patio.

Fire Fighter - "FIRE DEPARTMENT!!! One of your
neighbors called and   said you had a *huge* fire
in...your...back...uh...yard...and...uh...I see you
are...uh...getting ready to grill
some...er...food."

Smokey Brown – "Yes sir. I am."

Fire Fighter – "Well...uh...then...er...*never mind.*"

Curtain

Cast:

Smokey Brown – himself

City Fire fighter – him or herself

One of Smokey's Neighbors - ????????

Walk the Dog

I dunno. I guess I felt compelled to do it. I mean...it's 90 friggin' degrees outside...and I take the dog for a walk. My wife is on a short business trip so...as usual...I felt the need. It's not like Henri objects. No. At the sound of the word "walk" he perks his ears up...tilts his head as if those floppy, furry things are going to suck the preface "Do you want to take a..." right out of my mouth. That's what monsieur Henri wishes to hear. I obliged him.

The dog actually walks around holding the middle of his leash out for you to take. He's into it...big time. I remember a friend telling me that the best thing about having a small dog was that "all you have to do is run him up and down the stairs a few times." Meaning you didn't have to take him for a walk. And neither of us does that often. He runs around his backyard enough to salve any guilt.

So I took him on the usual yet not habitual route. It was around 6 in the evening. So people were out walking their dogs. And a lot of folks in the neighborhood have backyards with doggies frolicking. Bark! Bark! Bark! This is the yin and yang.

Dogs in yards. Bark! Bark! Bark! Dogs in the street. Sniff! Sniff! Sniff! If you're lucky that's how it happens. It's a little orchestral really, "Man's Best Friend Overture".

I only met a couple people on walks with their pooches. First there was a woman with two...she told me they were...um...well they looked to be Schnauzers but maybe terriers. My brain is no better with dog breeds than I am with human names. And that's pretty bad. The woman says, "Oh can we visit?" I assumed she was speaking about the dogs. Immediately one of her hounds was sniffing Henri's ears while the other one explored his "nether regions". Being a male Henri at first looked up at me like, "this is interesting...and perhaps...quite okay." But soon after I believe the two males...of which Henri was involved...realized the situation and began cautiously snarling at one another. The woman's male dog continued to bark in a very...very...focused dog kind of way as the French Boy and I soft shoed it out of there. I turned and walked backwards for a few yards watching her try to reason with a pedigree male dog. "Be good, boy! Be GOOD!" I yelled my apologies as I...with beast in tow...sashayed towards home.

The adventure was not over however. Just around the bend in the road appeared an older couple (and by that...now...in the year 2004...I mean "people about 8 years older than myself") that had what looked to be an Afghan Hound. They immediately turned their attention to Henri Richard...seemingly recognizing him...calling him Mazzy...Maggie...Mandingo. I dunno...something like that. They thought it was another dog by a name beginning with the letter "m" and were hard to convince otherwise. "In the green house over there lives a dog that could be...what's his name?"

"Henri" I replied.

"Well you should ring the bell there because these dogs are IDENTICAL!" By this point both their Afghan Hound...they called it by name but all I remember is being relieved the canine's moniker wasn't "Taliban" or something similar...and Henri were pulling their leashes in extreme excitement. I figured we had had enough "visiting" and bid the three ado. "He's so PRECIOUS!!!" the woman exclaimed. "He sure is...really PRECIOUS!!" the old guy yelled over at us.

As I headed in the direction of home with a panting...pulling...crazed Bichon leading the way, I glanced over my shoulder at the older couple (8 years?)...smiled...and said..."Yeah. He's precious all right. And it's a damned good thing!"

The Non-Fiction Theater of the Truly Mundane
proudly presents:

Philly Phone Call

Scene: Room 1201, Latham Hotel, Philadelphia, Pennsylvania, a classic European boutique style hotel. The room is modest yet tastefully decorated with a king sized bed, floor lamps, chest of drawers, heavy drapes and high backed Victorian reading chairs. Rick is sitting on the bed, lazily changing channels on the TV which sits...somewhat ill fittingly...in the corner by the bathroom door. Dressed for a late breakfast, he is waiting for Yvonne who is freshening up in the bathroom. The door is closed. They are in town for her nephew's wedding. Many friends and relatives have rooms in the same hotel...in Rick's mind...fortunately located on different floors. Rick appears somewhat bored.

The phone rings.

Rick saunters over to the nightstand by the bed and gingerly picks up the receiver.

Rick (in a confident tone) – "State Mental Institute!"

Mother in Law (seemingly confused...perhaps a bit

intimidated) -"Uh...uh...um...I was calling 1201?"

Rick – "This is 1201."

Mother in Law – "Uh...uh...is Yvonne or Rick there?"

Rick – "This is Rick."

Mother in Law – "Uh...this doesn't *sound* like Rick."

Rick – "Very well then. This is *BOB*!!!"

Mother in Law (excitedly and with a sense of deep
    relief) – "Now I *KNOW* this is *RICK*!!!"

Curtain

Cast:

Rick – Rick
Yvonne – anyone making "getting ready noises"
behind a closed bathroom door.
Mother in Law – Mother in Law

*This one act play is a true story. The names have been
kept the same to incriminate the guilty.*

Empty Palace

The weekend started off like so many others. Friday night we had friends over for dinner and conversation. Saturday we did chores and went out for a nice meal at a gourmet restaurant. And Sunday began like most stay at home weekends relaxing in the dining room reading the Sunday newspaper. My wife, Yvonne...unlike my life's desires...has maintained a successful business career. This is something I can't relate to on many levels. But hey...if she likes the challenge and enjoys her work more power to her. She works a lot of hours and because of this reads an entire week of newspapers on Sunday morning. We're usually up late the night before so Sunday morning coffee drinking and reading spills over into Sunday afternoon more times than not. That's the routine and we like it fine.

This particular Sunday was a little different in that we had tickets to see Tim Conway and Harvey Korman for the second of two shows at the Palace Theater downtown. The first performance was scheduled for 2 pm. We had seats for the "night" show, which was to start at 5 pm. For months we had been joking about the time of the show...that it was set up so we could all be tucked into beddie bye early. Korman and Conway have been around a while after all.

So it came as quite a surprise to me when Yvonne decided to give our dog Henri a hair cut...at 3:30 in the afternoon. Since we had spent the good part of 48 hours together I decided to dispense with the usual marital bickering and bite my lip. Now anyone who has been married for any length of time knows bickering at it's best can be a great communication device. At it's worst it can deteriorate into a full-blown argument. So after almost two solid days of congeniality I kept my silence.

Then I looked at the clock and saw it was 4:10. Yvonne...the blanket she was doing the haircut on...and the surrounding wall-to-wall carpeting...were all covered with dog hair. I'd venture to say there was more dog hair there than remained on Henri. I got out the vacuum and began sweeping the entire downstairs hoping this would be a clear signal as to the time situation. My lip was sore from my teeth clamping down on it. At 4:20 I figured it was time to throw caution to the wind. "Uh...you *are* aware the show begins at 5 aren't you?" Yvonne's head snapped around to the direction of my voice. Her eyes were filled with terror. "FUCK!!!" she cried.

Now my wife rarely swears let alone uses an f-bomb in front of anyone. She raced upstairs with the words "I won't wash my hair" lingering behind. This is a woman...who as a small child was nicknamed "Pokey" by her family. Yet much to my amazement there she was pulling her coat on at 4:40 saying "Let's GO!!!!" She drove. We made some lights. And I was astonished when we pulled into a relatively close parking garage at 4:55. It appeared as though we were going to have time to walk to the Palace Theater, score an expensive glass of cheap wine, and be escorted to our seat before the "fashionably late" came through the front doors. Incredible!

But I had an uneasiness come over me as we came up from the underground garage. "I know it's Sunday and Columbus isn't a bustling downtown...but doesn't it seem a little deserted to you? I mean...why would they have two shows if they only sold a couple hundred tickets for each one?" I said to anyone willing to hear...and they were few and far between. The wind whipped around us as we traversed the 2 blocks to the Palace Theater. The place had no one in front. Yvonne glanced over at me. And sure enough...once we got to the lobby entrance...taped to the doors...was a sign that read "Today's Shows Have Been Cancelled Due To Injury".

A little aside: this isn't the first time we've had this

happen. Twenty or so year ago we and a few friends piled into our 1964 VW Van and drove all the way to Cincinnati to see James Brown only to read a note that he was ill and the show postponed. We ended up shooting pool at a bar across the street for a couple hours.

"Geez...I hope one of them didn't fall down and break their hip." was the terribly ageist thought that popped into my brain." Yvonne turned around and we looked into each other's eyes. Serendipitously then...and I believe this may be a sign of "maturity"...we threw our arms around each other...threw our heads back...and laughed uproariously.

Sleepwalking

There was a short period of time in my life where I walked in my sleep. I'll call it that for lack of a better explanation. I was in my mid to late 30's I believe...a regular runner and generally obsessive exerciser. Whether that had anything to do with it I can't say. But it was the late 80's...the end of the Reagan years...and I approached narcissism just like most of the other people around me. Although I would like to think I kept a little humility back then. Not that we were as bad as the late 70's disco thing. But that's a story for a different day.

Actually I didn't really walk in my sleep so much as wake up doing irrational things. (Perhaps it was the bourbon I was fond of drinking back then.) Like trying to climb out the bedroom window. Or walking into my wife's closet at 4 am, knocking clothes off their hangers and waking her up. Then there was the time I waltzed into the bathroom and lifted the top of the clothes hamper thinking it was the toilet seat. Yvonne is a very sound sleeper. Yet she has this "take care of my stupid husband" radar that is impeccably psychic and accurate. I could write volumes about her saving my ass in the nick of time. But hey...that's for our 50th wedding anniversary and/or my funeral. Suffice it to say she managed that night to keep the dirty clothes from getting any dirtier.

Speaking of anniversaries...one time...I forget the year...we got ourselves a room downtown in a very nice hotel to celebrate such a calendar event. The two of us went out for a wonderful dinner where we ate and drank lots of wine and laughed and loved each other's company. Then we went back to our room where we drank lots of champagne and laughed and reveled in marital bliss and talked and drank more champagne. And laughed. And drank even more champagne. We eventually retired to the giant king sized bed and dozed off together...both au natural of course.

Sometime in the wee hours of the darkness...as is my customary nightly routine...I got out of bed to relieve myself. I didn't need to go badly...just enough to kick the sleepwalking thing into action. While my head was still euphoric from the champagne, I was barely conscious of my activity. I mean...I knew I was up but wasn't cognizant of where...what *time* it was...what *day* it was...what *year* it was...*where* I was. This is not an unpleasant feeling. Now that I have retired it is a daily occurrence...albeit a more conscious state of being.

Soon I walked through what I either did or didn't believe to be the bathroom door. It slammed behind me. I turned left and began trekking down a long, long well lit hallway. There were doors to my right and left identical to the one that just slammed behind me. And somehow I didn't find this at all curious. I continued to walk down the hallway…zombie like…until I got to a small lobby. There were elevators on either side of the room. And like most hotel floor elevator lobbies there was a table in between with a phone on it and a very large mirror above.

It was at this point in time reality started seeping back into my brain. I looked and saw my reflection in the mirror. My *nude reflection.* I was without a stitch of clothing…naked as …as…naked as a sunfish!! This didn't particularly strike me. In fact I thought, "All this running and working out has got me looking pretty *good!"* Yet I figured I had better hot foot it back to the room before I ran into some other sleepwalker. I glanced at the phone and thought, "I should call the room really. Tell Yvonne where I am. She might be worried." (I'm a good husband about such things…even when I am naked.)

But *what* room? What was the room *number*? What *was* that number again? I decided to head in the right direction hoping the sight of the correct number might bring it all back to me. 714? 785? I strolled for what seemed an eternity...774?...worrying about the number not coming to me when...all of a sudden...a door opened slightly. And arm thrust itself out and pulled me inside. It was Yvonne and her radar again.

Then we had this discussion...or something very close to it.

"What were you *doing* out there?"

"I thought I was going to the bathroom."

"In the *hallway*? You *unlocked* the door and walked down the *hallway*? You thought you were going to the *bathroom*?"

"Well...yeah...I guess."

"Did anyone *see you*?"

"I gotta pee."

Some marriages do not survive exploits such as these. No one did see me...not that in my state of mind I would have cared. But the hotel dick could have arrested me I suppose...dragged me down to the main lobby naked. But that didn't happen. And once again...Yvonne's radar saved the day...er...night.

An American in Paris

My wife Yvonne and I had spent an incredibly enjoyable week in the small village of St. Thibery in the South of France. The locals had been very friendly and our British hosts made us feel quite at home. Even the parade of tractors pulling wagons full of grapes en route to the winery every morning at the break of dawn was...in the long run charming...albeit an intrusion to our ever sleeping in. It was harvest time in wine country. Every five minutes or so a tractor would rumble past our open windows...wagons filled to the brim with harvested grapes...soon returning the opposing direction empty and hungry for yet another load. The scene was loud, intrusive, and joyous. Food, wine, baguettes, frommage and Chef Ben's 5 course meals made the experience all the more sensuous. I was saddened when we left.

After three adventurous days in Nimes, a small city full of fascinating relics of the Roman Empire, we took the bullet train to Paris for the last leg of what we scheduled as a celebration of my upcoming 50th birthday. (Okay, okay...so I've been partying since January 1st and the big day isn't until November 2nd.

It beats the hell out of moping around fishing for "Gee you don't look a day over 48" compliments doesn't it?) A swift cab ride took us to our hotel just 4 blocks from the Louvre.

Once inside our room I did what all men do after entering a hotel room...pick up the remote and turn on the television. And there it was. The image before me on the screen was one that I now share with probably billions of other people. "Holy shit! The World Trade Center is on FIRE!" I said in amazement to Yvonne who was busy getting settled. "Holy fuck! A plane just flew INTO the World Trade Center!" My first conclusion was that this must be some sort of bad made-for-television movie. But the image was on nearly all the channels...it seemed to be everywhere...French...German...British...American. Bad made-for-T.V. movies are NOT shown the world over...at least not at the same time. Yvonne was staring with me now. You know the rest...4 planes...buildings tumbling in their turns like houses of cards...thousands missing...thousands dead.

There is no way in hell I can explain what it felt like sitting in a Paris hotel room (an experience in itself I never thought I would have) watching this devastation on T.V. with French commentary...then German commentary...then British commentary...American commentary...back to

French. It was everywhere. The scene is burnt into my brain like so many in my lifetime before it: JFK, MLK, RFK, Kent State, John Lennon. Murder...murder...murder...murder. None of these events were accidents. Not one. An accident is sad...tragic. The space shuttle image was sad...tragic...still is. But murder is different...very much so. Murder. Different. Watching murder on television. On nearly every channel. When you've watched murder on television...the telly...you remember where you were. You remember who was with you. You remember what you said. You remember what they said. You remember numbness...all over. Blaring silence in your ears. Pounding in your brain. Screaming in your heart. A violent punch to your gut. A thousand words stuck in your throat like a murderous fish bone...a thousand murderous fish bones...stuck in your throat. You hear yourself breathe...watching others with no breath. No breath at all. This is how I felt. This is how I THINK I must have felt...all those times...all those murders. But I cannot be sure. I'm never sure...yet I'm VERY sure...always sure...this is how I felt. I'm sure...I think. Perhaps. I KNOW! Maybe...I think. This is how I felt sitting on the bed in the hotel room in Paris...surely...positively. I guess. Perhaps. Certainly. Yes. No.

Yvonne and I saw Paris. After all, we were on vacation. We walked everywhere. We saw as much as four days could give us. The Eiffel Tower. The Louvre. The Musee d'Orsay. The Arch de Triumph. The boulevards. The cafes. The people with their dogs...they love their dogs. The parks. The gardens. We loved Paris...everything about Paris. Loved it. Everything. Yet everywhere we went there it was. There it was again and again. The newspapers in the tobac shops. On the street corner obelisks. Memorial services at Notre Dame. At the Sacre Coeur. There it was. There it was again and again. I felt more American than I have in my entire life. A haunted American. Two haunted Americans...in Paris.

When our time ran out we went to the airport...just like you do when your vacation is over. Time is up. You go home. But at the airport...there it was again...there it was again and again...a hundred fold...a thousand fold. I had fallen in love with Paris with the woman I love...and yet I wanted to leave. I desperately wanted to go home. And I did...23 hours of security...insecurity...searching of bags...searching of souls...23 hours...security...insecurity...23 hours...later. I left. I came home. I came home...and...there it was. There it was again. There it was again and again. We both were home...Yvonne and I...we were HOME! And there it was. There it was again and again.

I'll go back. I'll go back again. To Paris I mean. Again. I'll go to Paris with the woman I love...again. Only the next time I go...to Paris I mean...I hope it is just Paris. Only Paris. And when I leave for home...I hope...with all my American heart...I hope...when I get home...when we're both at home...I hope it's just home. Only home.

A Rose by Any Other Name

One of the very best things about working at a large university is the influx of international students. Especially in the library, where I spend most of my waking time, there is no shortage of diversity. Several years ago I worked in close proximity with an attractive young woman from Spain. Her name was Carolina (pronounced "Care oh *leen - ah*"). She was vivacious, fun loving...and like most Europeans...well traveled compared to her American classmates.

While at work one fine day I was in a particularly jovial mood...for a change...when I noticed Carolina sorting books for re-shelving. I smiled at her and...using my best Curly Howard impression (which isn't very good) I shouted in her direction, "What's shakin' toots?" She stopped what she was doing...gave me a curious look...then swiftly walked up to where I was standing. Appearing perplexed...not at all angry...she leaned towards me and whispered, "Did you just call me 'tits'?"

I immediately realized the inherent danger a miscommunication such as this might befall me in this the 21st Century. "No! No! No! Of course I didn't call you 'tits'!" I emphatically replied. I patiently spent the next five minutes or so trying to explain first who the Three Stooges were. This went only a little better than the time I was telling her about the cookie loving...always begging...floating through the air with satisfaction after devouring a biscuit...cartoon dog from "Quickdraw McGraw" called Snuffles. But hey...most Americans don't remember Snuffles. Surely the Stooges had a worldwide reputation. Well...perhaps 50 years ago they did.

Secondly, I gave Carolina a history lesson that could have been titled "American Slang from the 1930's and 40's". "Toots" is an old slang term like "dame" or the more modern "chick", I told her. She looked quizzically into my eyes. "I was merely using an archaic term of endearment to say hello to you. It has nothing to do with body parts. I was just being funny. The word is 'toots'. It's like 'cutie' or something like that."

Carolina pondered this for a moment. There was no anger in her face...just contemplation...a mulling over of the word "toots". She then looked directly into my eyes...smiled wryly...in a somewhat nonplussed sort of way...and cheerfully proclaimed for all to hear, "It's okay. You can call me 'tits'!"

A Dog Day

It was one of those mid-summer days where the temperature is magnified by the exclamation point that is humidity. A day when the sun beats down and makes the air seem as thick as Jell-o. Dog days as they say. And while it would have been wiser to mow the lawn at say...10 o'clock in the morning...I managed to lollygag the morning away. Appropriately I was in the company of my dog, Henri...a French Boy of the Bichon Frise persuasion...and a lover of the great outdoors.

Henri insisted on joining me outside while I mowed. It is for all intents and purposes HIS yard. Been that way since the day I brought him home as a tiny ball of frenzied fur. He perched himself on the deck overlooking his kingdom while I filled his water bowl, then made my way to the garage and my mower.

Cutting grass behind the garage, along the sidewall...Henri's presence is always apparent. Many times he peeks his little face under the fence. I caught him doing this as I mowed...always thinking to myself, "What a charming little guy" or "He's so

DAMNED cute!" Only in the front yard am I alone with my task, sweating like John Henry laying down railroad track...but not for long. Again, as I move to the east side of the house there he is again...the white furry face with the tiny black nose and eyes peering adorably at me from under the six-foot tall fence. It melts my heart every time. Adorable. Henri is precociously precious...at times cocking his head as I speak to him...as if he is hanging on my every word. "Watch out for the gate boy!" I yell to his head tilting adorableness.

As I move into the backyard I see the pooch scramble up the deck stairs, panting from the heat. He barks at me and stares at the backdoor. Needing a break from the scorching sun myself, I let him in and get myself some ice water. I'm not sure whether to drink it or pour it all over me. The air conditioning feels like heaven. Henri plops himself down on the cool hardwood floor of the back room.

"Are you coming back out?", I inquire as if he were another human being. Henri just looks at my dripping self and sighs a big dog sigh, "No.". I can't blame him. I have no idea what the temperature is outside...just that it's hot as hell. Out to the yard I plod for some solitary sweating. I remember an old joke about the first man on the sun.

"Ouch! Ouch! OW!" (While the comic grabs his feet

one at a time hopping around) Corny…but a funny and apropos sight gag for this dog day and chore.

My final phase of mowing involves moving the hammock so I can mow where it sits. The lawnmower shuts itself off as I stride over and pull the rope leisure bed out of the way. It's then that I notice Henri perched on the loveseat in the backroom gazing at me through the picture window. Is that a forlorn smile on his doggie face? Surely he wants to rejoin me. So I walk back into the house.

"Henri buddy! Do you want to come outside and watch daddy finish mowing your yard?" I croon saccharinely. He wags his tail and swiftly makes his way past me while I hold the door open for his exit. And as I step down from the deck onto the patio I see my handsome little macho friend saunter over to my lawnmower…lift his back leg as high as he can…and pee all over it. Then, he hastily runs to the backdoor and barks his intension of the comfort of central air.

Underwater Jesus

I really didn't savor the idea of sweating by the pool for three days in upper 90's heat...not just at the Marriott Key Largo. So to put a unique stamp on this adventure I convinced Dan we should go snorkeling...in search of the "Underwater Jesus". I kid you not...there is a statue of Christ by a reef at the John Pennecamp Coral Reef State Park. I learned of this before the trip and it became somewhat of a personal pilgrimage. Not so much because I thought I'd be moved by an "Underwater Jesus", as that the idea struck me as totally weird. Little did I know exactly how weird the experience would be.

Dan and I drove to the state park on Friday to check things out...debated for the good part of the afternoon while lying by the pool in 99 degree weather...and decided to take the plunge the next day at noon. I do believe I piqued Mr. Eley's interest with my obsessing over "Underwater Jesus"...even though there was no guarantee that's where the state park's boat would take us for an hour of snorkeling.

Saturday was a LOT more crowded at Pennecamp than Friday. At first we lamented not going the day before...until we saw all the women getting on our boat. I'm not going to lie to you. Much of the attraction of going to the beach...the pool...anywhere hot with water...for a lot of healthy guys it's the almost naked women. The boat was full of young couples...and Dan and I. And even if we don't really qualify...we've been to the Florida Keys together before...so we're used to people assuming we're a gay couple. Why let it bother us? Both of us are used to it by now really. In the past we've been "gay fishermen". Today we were "gay snorkelers". Besides...it makes it less obvious we're ogling women more than half our age.

The crew consisted of two Park Rangers who gave us a tutorial in what to do if you thought you were drowning. I wasn't quite sure if either one of them had the athletic ability to save anyone...but I took their word for it. And the inflatable vest keeps a snorkeler afloat anyway...unless of course panic is involved. But Dan and I both have experience swimming and snorkeling. So I was relaxed...ready...excited even...for an audience with "Underwater Jesus"!!! And much to our delight one of the rangers announced that we were in fact, going to see the statue of Christ! Shiver me timbers and Holy Moses!!! We learned more...that the world has three statues like this. And Jesus is made from brass. He used to get polished all the time, which made him "glow" on a sunny day. But since the EPA recently made a rule that no one can touch coral in or around a coral reef the statue now has coral growing on it. "Underwater Jesus" is an integral part of the reef in this sense. He's covered with "Christaceans"!!

After an uneventful boat ride that lasted an hour, accompanied by the ranger's chatter, we dropped anchor and were ready for whatever lie beneath the surface. Across from us was a group of young Cubans...maybe four couples. And as everyone began stripping down to their swimsuits I saw that the Cuban women had on teeny, tiny, microscopic bikinis. Bikinis *so small* they could have been assembled from three Post Its and 6 inches of kite string! If "Underwater Jesus" wasn't smiling now...I was sure he would be in a few minutes...assuming he's...uh...straight of course.

So down the ladder I'm slogging with my flippers flapping...snorkel mask in place...breathing tube clenched between my teeth...and a guy who is already in the water quietly tells me, "Be gentle as you get in. There's a big barracuda about three feet from you...under the boat." Whoa boy!!! There's no easing in to this. Now I *know* a barracuda won't hurt you. *Intellectually* I know this. But if you've ever seen one up close...in the water...three feet away with nothing between the two of you...well...it can be a little intimidating.

Dan and I stuck together. He was manning his underwater digital camera and I was floating. It was a little choppy on this day. Fish were everywhere. The visibility was pretty good and the coral was easily admired as well. Soon enough...after we zoomed over a rise in the reef...there he was!!! "Underwater Jesus"...all seven feet of him...stood on a base in some 30 feet or so of depth. Arms up stretched...eyes looking for the surface...a beseeching look on his face...he seemed to be trying to tell us something...imploring us. Maybe it was chiseled in the base below his feet. I couldn't see. I could only imagine something like: First Neptune...chapter three...verses 17 through 22, "BLUB! Blubbibby blubbiby Blub!! Bluubby Blub Blub!!!" Of course this is in the original "Atlantis". The King James translation is "Truly, truly, I say unto you snorkelers!! I used to be able to WALK on this stuff!!!"

Okay...there's another week in Purgatory. And here comes yet *another*...because as I'm swimming...snorkeling...around "Underwater Jesus" (it was almost impossible to get away from him) I would occasionally look somewhere and see...some beautiful young Cuban female buttocks!! Hey! There's Jesus! Now there are the amazingly gorgeous buttocks of a young woman!! Hey…there's Jesus again!! Bare buttocks!! Jesus! Sweet Jesus there are those lovely young female buttocks again!!! This was… to say the least…quite disconcerting. Had there been an "Underwater Mary" as well, the scene would have been…metaphorically of course…Catholicism in a nutshell. (Seashell? Taco shell?)

It was then two epiphanies were revealed to me. The first…that I was getting mildly sea sick in the choppy waters. I began feeling somewhat queasy. The second epiphany…that if women had nipples on their buttocks our Puritan past would have incited some man to make them cover up…that I would not be gazing on the beauty of God's handiwork…some 15 feet from a statue of Jesus…underwater. No sir. I would be looking at some male invention called an Ass Bra instead!!! At this point in time I felt relatively delirious and told Dan I needed to get back in the boat. And after settling in onboard I began feeling even worse. Ironically, right across from me one of the pretty Cuban women commiserated with a crooked smile that said…in any language…I *too* feel like death Mr. Half of The Only Gay Couple on The Boat!!

Once on dry land I began feeling a little better. And as the day wore on Dan and I resumed our routine of sun, conch fritters, fish dip, oysters, beer and/or margaritas. And since we had a late check out Sunday we went to the pool for a while. Again, it was 99 degrees. I overheard a pool guy talking...telling others to begin tying the chaise lounges to the palm trees. I knew then it was time to leave. We missed Hurricane Rita sweeping over the Keys by maybe 30 hours. Fortunately its damage was minimal compared to Katrina. And Dan and I again celebrated our 30 some years of friendship. We felt lucky for that...for the adventure of "Underwater Jesus"...for missing the hurricane...and perhaps most of all...for women not having nipples on their buttocks!!

Big Bear Adventure

So I had to stop in at the Big Bear after work yesterday to pick up a couple prescriptions for my allergies. I despise Big Bear. It used to be a local chain of sorts (but no longer) so rather than give my money to the evil Kroger Corporation I started going there years ago. I hate everything about the place...the "kill or be killed" parking lot...the automatic doors...the fakey looking produce that shines like a newly polished brass spittoon...I mean EVERYTHING. And why do grocery store have to be named after wild animals or such? Is it a subconscious desire to go buy some prey in the glare of fluorescent lights? Groceries are named after bears, eagles, and lions. Why? Why not Enormous Antelope? Or Awesome Ape? "Hey! I'm going over to the Gargantuan Gazelle for some beer!"

Anyway, I sauntered up to the pharmacy and asked about my drugs...and ...of course...they aren't finished doing whatever it is they do that takes 45 minutes. Even though I had called 20 minutes earlier the pharm tech was frantically pushing the little Claratin pills up and down, up and down on his little tray. I have no idea why this is done. Maybe the pills need to be dizzy so they'll go in the bottle peacefully. I dunno. Since it's going to "be a few minutes" I decided to head over to pick up a six pack of beer instead of standing around looking at stuff that makes me feel old...like those $15 reading glasses I can't live without anymore. (although they work fine most of these specks look like they were designed in the 19th century...and you'll never lose them...they're too ugly to lose. I've had the same pair for five years running.)

I get my beer...walk back...pay for my prescriptions and head for the "express" line to buy my brewskis. After standing in the "express" line for at least 10 minutes waiting for the guy in front of me to have his "convenient" debit card approved, I finally get to the cashier. She looks directly at me and says, "You're going to think I'm crazy but I'll have to see a picture ID for that beer." To which I intelligently replied, "Say whu?" Of course I had left my driver's license in the car. Since I'm turning the big 5-0 later this year I guess I found the situation a little flattering. Still...I may look 40 on a good day but certainly NOT 20. So I said to the cashier, "You mean to tell me I can buy prescription drugs without a picture ID but I can't buy a six pack of beer?" "That's right" She says.

Being a bit frustrated albeit bemused...I head for my car....sans beer. On the way out through the "automatic" door I see an older gentleman sitting nearby and he looks up at me and asks, "Would you like to make a donation to help us win the war on illegal drugs?" To which I cheerfully quip, "Are you kidding? I'm going home to use some right now!" He gave me this look...the same one the assistant principal used to give me in high school after I said something. You know...it's that "Think you're pretty funny don't cha?" look. Oh well. Some people have no sense of humor. Hey...the guy at the carry out thought it was funny a few days ago...and today I'm feeling like a not-so-old smart ass.

The Non-Fiction Theater of the Truly Mundane

proudly presents:

Flu Shot

Scene: a large auditorium lobby on a major college campus.Tables with blank medical forms waiting to be filled out. Dozens of people (most in short sleeves) in a relatively straight line, filling out forms waiting to see one of three nurses at the line's end. Main character Rick waits in line until he is called back to the farthest nurse's table.

Nurse: Please sign this form. Have you ever had a flu shot before?
Rick: Yes. A few years ago. They ran out last year.
Nurse: Yes we did. Which arm do you want it in today?
Rick: My left arm already hurts. Let's do the left.
Nurse: So your left arm can be *totally* miserable?
Rick: It's not going to hurt *that* much is it?
Nurse (grinning and shaking her head from side to side): Oh no, no, no, no!!! Just a little stick. Now relax

your left arm. That's *wonderful!!* You relaxed so *easily!!!*

The nurse stabs the upper part of Rick's left arm. Rick grimaces slightly. She puts the syringe down and begins preparing a small band-aid for Rick's arm. The nurse drops the small, round band-aid.

Nurse: Ooooo!!...these tiny band-aids are *such* a pain in the *HOO HOO!!!*

The nurse picks up another bandage and begins peeling the backing off. She looks directly into Rick's face and smiles devilishly.

Nurse: You *know*...the HOO HOO? You know...the *HOO HOO...riiiight?*
Rick (earnestly deadpanned): Yeah...sure...I know the *HOO HOO!!!*

Curtain

Cast:

Rick - Himself
Nurse - Herself
Crowd - Themselves
HOO HOO - Hooself

Shipwrecked

Or

Faster! Faster Catfish! *Kelp! Kelp!!*

Saturday, June 23rd, 2007. 3:27 p.m. Hummingbird House, Tortola, BVI

My laptop's battery ran down Thursday so I couldn't write any more until the generators were turned on and I could recharge it. By then it was late Thursday night. Late that afternoon we made plans to go along on a dive boat so we could snorkel while the divers checked out the Rhone shipwreck. We were told on a sunny day snorkelers could see part of the wreck. I had my doubts about this but figured what the hell. We'll see some cool fish and coral anyway.

So Friday morning we sauntered up to the dive dock where two young women named Andra and Megan told the group...8 total with Yvonne being the only other woman besides the guides...how it was going to happen. Andra first off told us the name of the boat...which I forget...something stereotypically tropical like "The Calypso". And when I heard her say it was "26 feet long" I thought, "We're going out on the ocean in a TWENTY SIX FOOT BOAT?? But I eased my mild concern by reminding myself the Sir Francis Drake Channel is the easiest sailing in the WORLD!!! The calmest waters ANYWHERE!!! Besides...my father was in the U.S. Navy.

Still...I flashed back to my almost seasick snorkel trip with buddy Dan on Key Largo in the Florida Keys a couple years back. Then there was a much bigger group...maybe 30 or more...consequently we had a much larger vessel. Not to mention the protection from "Underwater Jesus" and the young Cuban women in incredibly small bikinis that helped take my mind off my stomach.

I again invoked the name of Sir Francis Drake for solace.

It took only about ten minutes to reach our mooring. And as Megan described the map of their dive I became acutely aware of the rolling waves...the bobbing of our "Calypso". My tummy began to dance. "Not to worry!!" I assured myself. All would be fine once I had my mask on and my face in the water.

Yvonne and I opted for wearing life jackets. Unfortunately, our fearless leaders had forgotten the snorkel vests that are effective and tidy. So we hung the big orange horseshoe pillows around our necks, took our instructions and slid off the edge of the

"Calypso". We both began swimming in the direction of the Rhone...or at least where we hoped it might be. The water was more than choppy. The depth was deep. I could see divers making their ways up and down their respective guidelines but no ship. I surfaced and yelled over to Yvonne...asking her if she saw anything. I immediately got smacked in the face with what seemed to be a three-foot tsunami...a liquid salt lick slapping me across my face. I coughed...and gagged a little.

"Are you okay?" Yvonne asked. "I do not feel too well out here." I replied.

"Then let's try over closer to shore. By the rocks. It will be calmer over there" She sounded so reassuring and I felt like I could...at the very least...make it through 40 or 45 minutes of snorkeling and then just relax in the boat for the remainder of the morning. And here there was no "Underwater Jesus" to save me. (I mean...who is going to hurl in the presence of the Lord?)

So we made our way towards the shoreline with the promise of calmer seas still ringing in my ears. It was about this time I realized my life jacket was behaving more like a "nerf noose" than anything having to do with the preservation of my being. My mind raced Shakespearean. "What fate dost thou choose? The gentle closing of thy throat sir? Or the allure the sea sirens? Mermaids with the promise of impossibility?"

Obviously I was having oxygen flow issues. I realized we were still many yards from shallower water when I turned to address Yvonne, got a mouth full of salt water, and before my brain could process "Here it comes!"...about halfway through the word "Here" really...MWOWW! Underwater Jesus...meet Underwater Ralph. At the age of 55 it's not everyday one has an experience they have never had before. Today was my day. Underwater upchucking!! I had no IDEA I was an "Underwater Upchucker Virgin"!!! Soon enough I was coughing and then...BWWOOOOWW!!!!!! But from now on I was determined to vomit in the air...you know...so the folks on the boats around me could enjoy the spectacle!! Then I noticed the look on poor Yvonne's face. That look that says, "My God! I have NEVER seen THAT before!!! And I really do not want to witness it again...." BBWWOOOWWW!!

My head felt like a chum bucket with a turbo projection option.

I don't know how many times I spewed. A person is so taken aback by the aquatic dimensions of barfing underwater, in the water, above the water...that I lost count. I'm guessing 8...in the water and it's vicinity. BBWWWOOOWWW!!! There are maybe 7 boats surrounding me while I gave this Chicken of the Sea performance.

I managed to get back to the Calypso...mostly through the help of tugboat Yvonne (It's times like these when I am dead certain this woman loves me.) I climbed onboard and realize one of the divers had given up the ghost already...before me!! A morale victory I suppose. But he wasn't sick. He was enjoying chatting with Andra. I would have too had I not had to use everything in my strength to try to keep my secret (I hoped) Underwater, Above Water, In the Water Upchucking reputation in the past.

But no...it was not to be. As soon as ALL the divers were onboard ...there I was hanging helplessly over the side of 26 foot Calypso dry heaving like there was no tomorrow.

"I'm feeding the fish" I joked as soon as I realized everyone was aware.   "

"Someone has to!!" Megan added for levity.

And Andra asked me if I wanted to go back. There was an hour wait before the divers were allowed to go back into the water. And she could take me back. Did I want to go back to terra firma?

Did I ever.

Puck

I enjoy a good baseball game...the summer weather...the cold beer...the crack of the bat. And I've always wanted to catch a foul ball...or a home run. But considering my career as a ballplayer when I was a boy, my more realistic goal is merely to get a baseball...pick it up off the floor...out of a seat...after it has eluded everyone else in the near vicinity.

I played (and I use the verb very loosely) in what was known as Summer League in my hometown. Unlike *the official* Little League, no one was cut. Every boy had to play the field two full innings and bat at least once to constitute a fair, authentic game. Fair – yes. Equitable – hardly. I might have had a happier childhood had I been cut from the team...or merely sat on the bench the entire nine innings. My first season I went all summer without a hit...or a catch for that matter. 0 for 1000 perhaps. The pitchers were so bad too. I struck out, walked, or got hit with the ball. When a kindly coach had the brilliant plan to develop me into a left handed hitter due to my bad left eye, I got hit in the head with enough fastballs that I begged him to let me strike out from the right side of the plate where I was comfortable at sucking.

I was no better in the field. Bad players were put at second base with the intention of the shortstop hogging grounders hit anywhere near second base. *Really* bad players were banished to right field and everyone on the team...including myself...prayed to God Almighty no one would hit it out there. This is when I began doubting the existence of God...the first time a screaming line drive was hit at me. My well intentioned coach tried his hardest to get me to conquer my fear. "What's uh matter Brownie? You 'fraid the ball is gonna hit you in the face or sumthin'?"

"Why yes...yes I am sir."

I fared a little better in football...at least on defense. But when the starting quarterback came up to me and said, "Brown, you run great patterns. Better than anybody on the team. But you never *catch* the goddamned *ball!!*" I decided my artistic ability was probably going to be my mainstay after that comment and promptly quit the team...which regardless of what a lot of men will tell you...is quite a liberating experience.

So finding a baseball has always been my goal. Trouble is this can be a vicious scene. I've witnessed young boys knock down a gimpy old man, racing to get a ball bouncing around the empty seats of old Cleveland Municipal Stadium. I've watched my buddy Karl turn into a crazed orangutan, leap in front of me, and gobble up a foul ball as if his life depended on it. The closest I have ever come was in a smaller minor league park when a ball jettisoned back towards me and hit the pole to my immediate right. So almost getting killed by a line drive foul is my nearest accomplishment.

My wife's company has season tickets for the Columbus Blue Jackets (what a ridiculous name for a hockey team) and the other night four of us were treated to the seats. Now these are not your ordinary sporting event seats. These are right down on the glass where it's so cold you keep your (blue) jacket on. They are aisle seats. Sitting this close one gets to see a lot of smooshed hockey player faces as they smash each other relentlessly into the Plexiglas. It's really cool...even if...like myself...you couldn't give a rat's ass about hockey.

Sometime in the third period I catch a disturbance to my immediate left...like a mini-riot or something. These incredibly large (I'm being nice here) men dressed in hockey jerseys (which do *not* have any slimming effect at all) are trying desperately to rise out of their seats, to bend over, to reach out. And they are grunting and caterwauling. Suddenly...to my amazement...I see a small back circular thing pop out from under the fray and begin to roll...ever so gingerly...but with seemingly purposeful intent...across the aisle step towards me. Like Shakespeare's muse this Puck did glide in my direction as the crowd on my left groaned and grunted in their cramped immobility. With a nonchalant confidence I have rarely known, my left hand reached down, snatched the cold black treasure from its exhilarated escape and thrust it in the air for all to see! Like a trophy from the gods I held it high! I then bit Puck....as if it made from solid gold...just to make sure the moment had actually occurred. Because, as you see, this was the very first...and possibly the final...athletic play I had ever made. In an effort to salve the pain of the large, yet mere mortals to my left, I tried in vain to contain my pride.

And although it is not a baseball...this Puck...*my* Puck...makes for one hell of a paperweight.

The Non-Fiction Theater of the Truly Mundane

proudly presents:

Senior Excursion!

Act One

Scene: a small, almost filled mini-bus with 9 senior citizens mostly sitting towards the back of the vehicle. Driving is a young woman with Rick sitting directly behind her, riding along to learn how to be a back up driver. It is a bright, brisk sunny February day, late morning.

Driver – I don't know who ordered this beautiful day but thank you! The sun is   wonderful!
Senior Lady #1 (from the middle of the bus) – It's gonna *RAIN* tomorrow!
Senior Lady #2 (from the very back of the bus) – And it's gonna *SNOW* Thursday!
A guy named Bob – Where are we goin' after lunch?

Driver – Shopping at a couple used clothing stores. Won't that be fun Bob?

A guy named Bob – I don't need nothin'! Got all I need. Don't need nothin'!

Rick – You never know Bob.

A guy named Bob – Everything! Got it!

Driver – Don't forget daylight savings time is coming up real soon...March 8th I think.

Senior Lady #3 – I don't understand what daylight savings time is *for*.

Senior Lady #2 – More light at the end of the day they say.

Senior Lady #4 – What does anybody need light at *night* for? Morning's when I do stuff! Night is supposed to be dark!

Senior Ladies #1, #3, #5, #6, #7 – Yeah! In the morning!

Senior Lady #4 – And what about the KIDS? Standing around in the dark! I never went to school when it was dark!

A guy named Bob – Me either! Went TO school when it was light...came *home from school when it was light!*

Senior Lady #7 – And what about the *FARMERS?!!*

Senior Lady #5 – And what about the ANIMALS?!!

A guy named Bob – Animals don't care...don't care about much of anything.

Curtain

Act Two

Scene: The parking lot of a local restaurant. Rick and
A guy named Bob are standing, waiting for the driver
to come out and open up the bus doors. The rest of
the group slowly drifts out of the restaurant. The sun
is still shining brightly.

A guy named Bob - What's your name again?
Rick – Rick
A guy named Bob – You have any of that pie in there?
      (Pointing to the restaurant behind him)
Rick – No. But it looked delicious.
A guy named Bob – Know how much a piece of pie
      was in there? (Pointing back to   the
      restaurant behind him)
Rick – No.
A guy named Bob – TWO NINETY FIVE A SLICE!
Rick – Is that a lot?

A guy named Bob looks at Rick incredulously while Senior Lady #4 walks up to him.

Senior Lady #4 – Hey Bob…did you have some pie? It was delicious!

A guy named Bob – How much did you *pay* for a piece of that pie?

Senior Lady #4 – Don't recall.

A guy named Bob – TWO NINETY FIVE! That's how much! A piece of pie used to be a DIME!

Senior Lady #4 – Oh.

She pauses and thinks for a moment.

Senior Lady #4 – Pie was never a dime.

A guy named Bob – 10 CENTS! Sure was!

Senior Lady #4 – Imagine how much a *whole pie* must cost.

A guy named Bob – I DON'T EVEN WANT TO *THINK* ABOUT IT!

Curtain

Cast:

Driver – Herself
Rick – Himself
Senior Ladies – Themselves
A guy named Bob – A guy named Bob

Sunday Night with a Monday Off

1:37 a.m

You know...people say early to bed and all that shit. But when the opportunity presents itself...I always promise myself I'm going to be disciplined...you know...drink and eat moderately. That's the easy part really. I can do that...when I'm alone...I mean me and the dog...I'm cool with THAT. But the going to bed at a reasonable hour thing...as they say...getting up early to make the most of "the day God has given me"...I can't handle that crap.

And that's what it seems to be to me...crap. When it's 12:15 a.m. and I don't have to be anywhere before 3 p.m. tomorrow I just stay up late. Don't care what's on TV...doesn't matter...BAM! Emeril Live...that's cool enough. Or maybe Iron Chef...tonight it's a rerun of "Iron Chef - eels"!! And now with a fireplace and a fire to tend to...camping in the house...with TV...cool...much harder convincing myself. To sleep I mean. So I stay up even later...even the dog looks at me like...hey...I'm tired. But he loves the fire and comes around to my way of thinking. And there is something about defying the clock...the sun...the darkness...the norm driven into my head from elementary school about "responsibility"...all that arbitrary shit.

I'm not talking about dancing all night at a club...fantasizing about girls...or the empty promise of excitement...playing poker with the boys...or pinball at Dick's Den...pool at Larry's with the sawed off cue stick...tables too close to the wall. Home...late at night...early in the a.m. After midnight. That's suits me just fine. Just the calm...the darkness...the railing against what most think is normal and good. Celebrating daylight? Accomplishing? Let it go. Screw it. It's not that it turns me on...makes me feel validated or such...being indecisive about hours of sleep.

It's merely cozy...the lateness...the darkness...the stillness...the sleeping dog's sighs...the 57 channels and nothin's on. Kind of like getting up REAL early...for a walk with the dog.. Opposite and the same. That's great...but I don't want to do that. No motivation for morning...not tonight anyway...not most times. I'd rather be belligerent...immature perhaps...and stay up late...for no apparent reason whatsoever.

Maybe it's the dumb celebration of trying to relive age 12 again...when me and the pals slept on Don Chilcher's rec room floor...or tried hard not to...even if for just a couple hours or so... doing something against the rules. "Ripley's Believe It or Not" "Mad Magazine"...Beatles singing "She Loves You!"...all night. "It'll rot your brain"...bullshit. Yeah! Yeah! Yeah! Fun 'cause we knew that was parent's bullshit. Break rules...nothing big...just "not the right thing to do"...maybe that's it. It's still liberating. Fire...dog...BAM! Emeril. Up a notch. Still cool. Staying up late...watching dumb shit on the television.

Or writing this.

Insomnia

I glance at the clock. 3:45 a.m. At my side is my wife...snoring serenely in her delicious slumber, as if serenading her co-hibernating husband. I envy her inert unawareness.

Soon my mind is swimming...almost drowning in thoughts. Like popping kernels of cerebellum they explode into my consciousness...as if my head was the office microwave. Salted into these sometimes creative ideas are always the petty worthless worries. What time is it *now?* How many hours will I get if I fall asleep *right now?* Dinner tomorrow? The front door? The back door? The waitress? The car? The washing machine's newest noise?

Oh sure...I've tried all the relaxation exercises people talk about...the Zen of falling asleep from sleeplessness. Count sheep. Concentrate on your breathing. In...out...in...out. *Iiiiiin...ooooout.* POP! Didn't I just do this with the dog all evening? In...out? And the green light of calm...beginning at the toes...slowly climbing my body...mellowing myself in intentional increments. Still...as usual...by mid-shin...approaching the creaky knees...the green goes

POP!!! In my brain. Idea alert!!! Write this down! Others experience this right?!! No...wait...sleep...morning...won't I forget? I will...no...I won't.

Plan two...the new position. Right side. Left side. Back. Pillow fluff. My poor little dog accommodates my tossing/turning ballet with devoted assimilation. Curl up close...followed by two poochie snorts and a doggie sigh. On the last maneuver he patiently adjusts...does his routine...then rolls on his back in submission...passing what small alpha he can muster in the middle of the night to me with an implied, "Please. No more."

And finally I feel drowsiness returning. My eyelids relent. The popping thoughts slow. With my family surrounding me I have one final muse.

Life is *good*.

NO WAIT!!! JUST...*ONE MORE THING!!!*

Man...am I gonna be tired tomorrow.
Zzzzzzzzzzzzzzzzzzzzzzzzzzz

The Non-Fiction Theater of the Truly Mundane

proudly presents:

Almost 99

Scene: The driveway of a middle class urban neighborhood. A small community center bus is parked directly in front of a sidewalk that leads up to the front door of a small, immaculate, white two story frame house. An old fashioned lamppost is situated next to the walkway. Rick (the driver) is seen standing next to the open accordion bus doors. He is helping a little old lady out of the bus. Sitting inside are 5 other senior ladies.

Rick – Here we are! Do you need help getting out?
Little old lady – A little maybe. I'm going to be 99 on June 2nd you know.
Rick – Why yes. I heard you talking to the others about that. I think that's just wonderful!
Little old lady – Isn't it though.

She begins her decent down the bus stairs.

Rick – Now you watch this last step. It's a bit more of a drop than the others. It's a doozy really.
Little old lady – You know, this one time we all went to lunch. And one lady got drunk. And when she got to this last step she turned and looked at the rest of us. And do you know what she said Rick?
Rick – I have no idea.
Little old lady – She said "This last goddamned step is a BITCH!"

Curtain

Cast:

Rick – himself
Little old lady – her almost 99-year-old self

January 20, 2008: Retirement Day 21 Checklist of Accomplishments

Sunday Solitude

By Pajama Boy

Drove wife to the airport.

Mourned loss of Suzanne Pleshette on drive back.

Came home and put on blue plaid pajamas.

Let dog out.

Got newspapers off front porch. (Brrr – 20 degrees)

Built fire in fireplace. (red man's fire *)

Let dog in.

Read the New York Times. ALL of it.

Drank coffee.

Mourned death of Richard Knerr, co-founder of

Wham-O, company that introduced the Frisbee, Hula Hoop, and Super Ball.

Let dog out.

Ate bowl of cereal while standing watching Giada De Laurentiis on kitchen TV.

 Let dog in.

Gave dog cookie.

Talked to friend on phone.

Talked to wife on phone.

Let dog out.

Ignored 8 mystery phone calls.

Read the Columbus Dispatch. (Took 15 minutes)

Let dog in.

Emailed a little bit.

Let dog out.

Listened to classical music and opera.

Read from Connie Shultz's "*...and His Lovely Wife*".

Let dog in.

Horsed around with dog.

Let dog out.

Ate homemade soup.

Let dog in again and told him to "cut the shit".

Gave dog cookie.

Took shower.

Put on green sweatshirt, black sweatpants, blue socks, black sandals.

Poured Bakers 7 Year Small Batch Bourbon (on the rocks) and began sipping it.

Turned TV on to watch football

Let dog out.

Got leftover eggplant Parmesan out of fridge while 2nd guessing size of bourbon drink.

Let dog in and repeated "Cut the shit" empty threat.

Roughhoused with dog. (Somewhat different than

horsing around…involves dog "skootching" under master's arm.)

Gave dog reward cookie for superb "skootching".

Carried in firewood and initiated "white man's fire".

Let dog out.

Set oven for 375.

Let dog in.

Put dinner in oven.

Shielded dog from heat of white man's fire while watching football.

Ate dinner at halftime with glass of Chianti.

Gave dog cookie.

Cleaned up and let blaze downsize to red man's fire.

Stepped on one of 12 bones dog put in front of fireplace while returning to couch.

Caught balance, avoiding fall on floor.

Talked to wife on phone.

Resumed white man's fire.

Flipped between football and Iron Chef. Both contests close.

Let dog out.

Made coffee for morning.

Let dog in.

Missed end of Iron Chef while watching New York Giants win in O.T.

Watched Lewis Black on Comedy Channel.

Woke up on couch 20 minutes later.

Let dog out.

Let dog in.

as a young summer camp counselor I learned of a supposed Native American axiom that read: White man build big fire...stand waaay back. Red man build little fire...get way up close.

OOH LA LA!

Wednesday, January 16, 2008
10:37 a.m.

    I went to a French Bakery called La Chatelaine this morning to pick up some bread and this pretty...dark haired...late 40-ish woman with a "Donna" name tag, dressed in her French peasant dress smiles and says "Bonjour". I reply "Bonjour mademoiselle" and order a boulle..."s'il vous plait". So she pulls a boulle out of the appropriate basket and puts it in the slicing machine, slices the loaf, wraps it up for me and asks if I wanted anything else. I tell her "merci no."
    Then...as I'm giving her my money...she inquires,
    "Are you going to eat it now"?
    I must have looked quite surprised...perhaps even taken aback...because then she says, "The bread...it is very...fresh!"
    This kind of threw me for a loop...took me

out of my element I suppose.

    I stammered sheepishly, "Probably...uh...not until tonight."

    And in response...as she gingerly places the change into my awaiting palm, she smiles broadly at me and almost purrs, "Just one piece now perhaps...in your car. It is very...very...fresh."

And I thought...wow...she's flirting with me.

I may or may not have blushed.

Charming little vignettes like this...I mean...I've been thinking about her on and off all day...these are the good things in life. C'est bon.

A taste of my own medicine I suppose.

I don't even think she is French.

Don't care.

If the Bird is the Word Then Fish is the Dish!

One of the newest words in the dictionary this year is pescatarian. In fact, its so new spell-check doesn't recognize it! Now ordinarily I loathe labels. But after years of explaining that I'm a "vegetarian who eats fish"...meaning I'm not really a vegetarian at all, but merely lean far in that direction...it is a relief to have a word that brings all of us together. Asking, "Are you a pescatarian?" surely will cut down on a conversation's length. But think of the joyousness of finding someone who shares the same diet without all the linguistic logistics! It's as if we now belong to a special club that no longer makes us feel just a little bit the outsider.

Of course "a vegetarian whose diet includes fish" (the official definition) is a contradiction much like "a carnivore whose diet includes vegetables". But hey...they have had the word "omnivore" for a long, long time now. And it sounds a lot more official than veggivore.

Still, my exuberance is tempered by the word itself. I mean...it does sound remarkably like *Presbyterian* does it not? And I'm certain there are Presbyterian pescatarians...although I'm betting there are significantly *more* Unitarian pescatarians. And now that we are the pescatarians (We are the pescatarians! We are the pescatarians! No time for omnivores 'cause we are the pescatatians!! *Of the world!*) a Pandora's Box full of pressing questions prevail.

Such as the Christian symbol of the fish. You know...the one people slap on the back of their cars. Perhaps there should be a new, enhanced image for say a Unitarian pescatarian. My suggestion would be the current fishy symbol with Ms. Pacman...mouth wide open...waiting to pounce on Pisces! Many times while sitting in traffic this conundrum has always mangled my mind...is this THE Holy Mackerel? But hell, I figure there's no need putting my proboscis out of place over it.

And with the advent of a word exclusive of fish eating vegetarians, what if there are vegetarians who include only fowl in their diet? Say, only eat turkey at Thanksgiving...or just can't give up bird? Surely these people must exist and deserve a word for themselves as well. I suppose they could easily be Fowlists right? Let's not forget vegetarians who include reptiles in their diet! Would they be reptilarians? Or insects? Would they be insectarians? Why not? With all this specialization one could easily envision a room full of fowlists (some named Fowler?) squabbling about squab or grousing over grouse! We pescatarians can sometimes be heard carping about carp or squiddling over squid! Believe me!

Of course this also begs the moral question: Does a promiscuous pescatarian *snook* around?

Has anyone realized that a Pelican...or any fish eating bird...is also a pescatarian? "The bird is the word" must be in the Dead Sea Scrolls somewhere.

Life just keeps getting more complicated.

Just think of all the new possibilities in our world of dietary cultural labeling. I am by no means complaining. I think it would be great if the Pescatarian Proctologists Association adapted "To live to be an octogenarian, first become a pescatarian!!" as their motto!

So I embrace my new label. I celebrate my pescatarian values proudly!! Because in my heart of hearts I know...nudist pescatarians are most certainly loyal readers of Naked Sunfish!!!

The Non – Fiction Theater of the Truly Mundane

proudly presents:

King Crab Legs

Scene: A small gourmet market's seafood department. An upright freezer stands stage left. Center stage is a long, glass fronted seafood cooler displaying a myriad of fish, shellfish, et al. Behind the counter is Chuck the fishmonger doing his chores. He is wearing the market's shirt and matching ball cap. Rick approaches from stage right pushing an empty, red grocery cart. Rick stands in front of the fish counter waiting for Chuck's attention. Chuck, wiping his hands, notices Rick.

Chuck – HEY!!! How are ya? What can I do for you today?

Rick – Chuck, I need some crustacean advice.

Chuck – Sure thing.

Rick – I'm looking to buy some frozen Alaskan Kung
      Crab legs and had a couple   questions.

Chuck leads Rick over to the upright freezer stage
left, opens the door and pulls out two very large, long
crab legs wrapped in clear plastic.

Chuck – Here is a little over two pounds. Great, great
crab.

Rick – Would that be enough for two people?

Chuck – Oh yeah…sure.

Rick – And how do I prepare it?

Chuck – Just steam them until they're done…5, 6
      minutes…maybe a little more. When the shell
      turns orange you know they're done. Serve
      them with some melted butter. Great!

Rick (Taking the package from Chuck) Soooo…you're
sure this is enough for two.

Chuck – More than enough to wow someone. Are you
trying to WOW someone?

Rick – It's my wife's birthday.

Chuck takes a look around and when he sees there is

no on else nearby, puts his arm around Rick's
shoulder, smiles, and leans in close.

Chuck (Quietly yet earnestly) – Maybe you'll get *laid!*

Rick – That's what I was banking on!

Curtain

Cast:

Chuck – Himself
Rick – Himself
King Crab Legs – King Crab Legs

Walk the Dog II

When there is what appears to be more than two feet of snow lying on the ground I am certainly not inspired to go out in it. And luckily for me...being mostly retired...I don't have to very often. My wife drives our old 4-wheel drive Jeep Cherokee. So I manage to salve any guilt involved with her slogging her way to work every day because of that. Some days I'm more successful at this than others.

It's been a nasty winter...and it is by no means over yet. Central Ohioans seem to forget what winter is...until it arrives again the following year. Their driving is a testament to that. And again...I am grateful to no longer be forced to dodge minivans sliding sideways in the slush...children's faces pressed hard against frosty windows in horrifying terror.

But today...snowshoes or no snowshoes...pajamas be damned...I had to (are you ready for this?) take the trash out to the alley and the recycling out to what's known in milder times as the "tree lawn". I was gripped with fear until the "take the damned trash out" conversation with my wife and the "take the damned trash out" email from a friend.

Ordinarily...and by that I mean when there is not

what seems to be two feet of snow lying on the ground...my Bichon buddy strolls with me out to the alley...sans leash. It's a ritual called "Wanna Do TRASH? Will you be a GOOD BOY if we Do TRASH?" And upon my utterance of this proclamation...or the awareness that I am taking the big black bag out of the kitchen's trash bin...Henri goes ballistic! Barking...wagging his tail like it's going to fly off mid-wag. Today he was even more excited. My dog has cabin fever as much as I do.

So I put on warm clothes, a knit cap, scarf, gloves...the winter uniform. (Has it ever dawned on you that when it is severely cold outside you'll put anything on that's warm? Regardless of whether it matches or clashes? I like to say, "When it's cold you don't give a shit what you look like." Henri finally lets me put on his harness...there is no way I'm letting him go "off leash" since we won't see sidewalks until spring. We head for the alley...trash bag in one hand...Henri on the leash in the other.

And of course since the French Boy hasn't been on a walk for a while he's, running from one side to the other disregarding snow depth as if he didn't care. (He doesn't.) We made it to the trashcan, although it took us maybe 3 times longer than in the summer. I had not originally planned on going anywhere else but back to the house. But in the street about 20 yards from Henri and I stood a pretty young woman and her beautiful

Chocolate Lab. (Even if she was 40...and she wasn't...I'm old enough now that she would seem like a college girl to me.) What could I do? I HAD to behave like I was actually taking my dog for a walk didn't I? She smiled at us warmly and said, "Hi! Why don't you come over and let the dogs visit?"

Now Henri is not a mean dog. He is adorable. But he CAN be precocious and defensive...especially with other male dogs. I told her exactly that but she insisted our dogs "visit". And I thought that with all the snow in the street there was no avoiding it anyway. She did smile at us. Her dog appeared well-trained...calm. And maybe Henri would be congenial despite his surly cabin fever mood.

He was not.

But the pretty woman was nice. She understood. "It's okay" she kept saying. "Dog person" I thought. And as we were walking away I heard her soothingly ask her pooch "Were you afraid of that little guy?" I think he might have been. Henri had no doubts.

Around the block...that's all...around the block I figured. Since we were now obligated to take some sort of walk...at least in my own mind...and Henri's...that's what we did. We strolled around the block in mini-loge tubes that Henri unsuccessfully...on purpose...stayed within. And in the course of just one city block this little feisty dog must have peed 50 times! This was mildly annoying but somehow made me feel better about my own bladder.

But he pooped not once...not twice...but THREE TIMES!! All in a once around the block walk. And to be honest it crossed my mind that pooping in the snow...*on the snow*...might give me a certain satisfaction as well. I don't know how my neighbors would have taken it. Would they be disgusted? (I had a college roommate who referred to it as "the most disgusting of all human functions" and even had a "Poop Prayer". That being, "Dear God...*mmmm...mmmmmuh*...please make it come!" Either he was terminally irregular or just trying to be funny. It was hard to tell with him.) Or would my neighbors embrace it? Maybe cheer out their windows, "DEFILE THAT FUCKING SNOW!!! GO RICK GO!!"

My modesty...well...actually my experience both in winter backpacking and fantasy always better left fantasy...brought me to my senses. I simply guided my canine companion home. Once there I realized today's epiphany had nothing to do with pooping. No. Not even on the snow. No. It's that it's a good thing I'm happily married. Because I'd *never* get lucky with THIS dog at the end of my leash.

The Non Fiction Theater of the Truly Mundane

proudly presents:

Multiplex Movie Matinee

Scene: The lobby of a large urban multiplex movie house. A group of senior ladies sit alongside the wall stage left. Their drivers (Rick and Ken) are leisurely standing opposite them along with two young female social workers. They are chatting about the movies the senior ladies have just finished seeing.

Rick – So what did you ladies see today?
Senior lady #1 (excitedly) – I saw "Julie and Julia".
       Walked in just as the trailers were ending. It
       was a lovely film. Now I'm starving!
Rick – And how about the rest of you?
Senior lady #2 – We all saw "All About Steve" and it was pretty good.
Senior lady #3 – For *today's* movies it was.
Senior lady #4 – Yeah...they don't make movies like they used to.

Senior lady #3 – You're right there. Don't make *anything* like they used to!

Just then two elderly gentlemen emerge from a theater door at the back of the stage. They slowly walk up to the group.

Ken – What did you guys see today?
Senior guy – Something called "Whiteout".
Rick – Oh. The blizzard flick huh? What did you think?
A guy named Sam – I couldn't *tell* if it was any good! Too much damned snow! I couldn't even see the actors!! Way too much damned snow!!
Senior guy – How would you know Sam? You *slept* through most of it.
Senior lady #5 (incredulously) – He *slept* through the *movie*?
Senior lady # 2 (also surprised) – You *slept*?
A guy named Sam – I did *not* sleep through the movie! I was too damned cold!
Senior guy – Did too!
A guy named Sam – Did NOT!
Senior guy – Did SO!
A guy named Sam – NOT!
Senior guy – You did TOO!
A guy named Sam (pondering for a moment) – Well...maybe...a *little* bit...at the end.

Curtain

Cast:

Rick – himself
Ken – himself
Social workers – themselves
Senior ladies – themselves
Senior guy – himself
A guy named Sam- A guy named Sam

Stacy's Buffet

Prologue: This is a true story. The names have been changed to...uh...well...I'm not really sure why I'm changing the names; to protect the innocent perhaps. Or maybe I'm calling the lead character Edith simply because she reminds me so much of my late aunt. I'm keeping my name the same. There's nothing particularly innocent about me. And you'd figure it out anyway.

The community center I work for, as a part time driver, is like most social agencies I've had experience with. By that, I mean it's wonderfully unorganized. So in early December came the realization that too few excursions had been planned for the year and funding would be lost if a few more weren't added. I signed up to drive seniors to a cafeteria called Stacy's Buffet. I had no idea the adventure that would unfold.

One thing I've learned about seniors is that they will ask you to take them to the Olive Garden 30 miles away...even though there is one only 5 miles down the road. At first I thought this odd. Are the bread sticks longer there? I mean...every Olive Garden is the *same* isn't it? "But we haven't been to THIS one" they'd say. Sooner or later I realized the longer the trip, the better. It was the journey more than the destination. Almost every senior I'd met felt this way...until I met Edith.

Stan, the other driver, was to pilot the 14-passenger bus while I took "Big Red". "Red" is an aging Ford Econoline Van...a comfortable albatross...and this was to be my virgin excursion in it. I chuckled when I saw the schedule and the plan was to meet at Stacy's for dinner...at 4 in the afternoon. The "Early Bird's Early Bird Special" I suppose. And because Edith used a 4-wheeled walker and lived across the river at an assisted living facility, I had only two others. And they lived on their own. I knew Don...a nice man who smoked cigarettes with the intensity of a greaser behind the high school between classes. I was also familiar with Edna...an elderly, stoned faced woman who mostly sat in chilling silence.

Stacy's was not remotely a short drive. Best-case scenario, the trip would take 45 minutes each way. So, when I heard the weather report of possible sleet and temperatures in the mid 30's I felt somewhat anxious. I climbed in Big Red at 2:30 and headed to

Edna's apartment building. I honked the horn and shortly she made her silent, almost zombie like trek down her sidewalk and into the middle seat of the van. Don was a few minutes away and as I pulled into his parking lot I saw him standing in front of his door, frantically sucking in the last hits from his cigarette. The two of us exchanged pleasantries and he took the front seat next to mine.

Don and I chatted for most of the 15-minute cruise to Edith's place. I pulled up close to her apartment's door and she emerged, a little hunched over yet persistently pushing herself along with her 4-wheeled walker. This was my first time meeting Edith and I was polite and cheerful.

"Hello Edith! We're going to Stacy's Buffet today!" I yelled.

"I gotta sit in the front seat! Can't get into the back! I'm using a walker ya' know" she seemed to snarl.

Don was congenial about giving up his seat and took his place way in the back. As I helped Edith into the van, I immediately realized that my personal space was getting a radical makeover.

"And nobody better be SMOKING on this trip 'cause if you even come CLOSE to me with smoke you will have to take me to the emergency room!" Edith barked.

I assured her that no one would be smoking in the

vehicle and thought to myself, "THIS is why I'm driving PART time!"

The original plan was for Stan's people and mine to meet at Stacy's so everyone could eat together...or at least within a similar time frame. You know...dinner at 4 o'clock. But the weather already began to turn lousy. There was a steady drizzle as I pointed Big Red east towards what was supposed to be Buckeye Lake but turned out to be Heath...which is 20 miles *north* of the lake. How this happened is beyond me. I guess the unorganized is not ALWAYS wonderful. I tried calling Stan. His phone was dead.

About 20 minutes into the excursion...and we've been out of the city for a good 10 miles now...Edith turns to me and says, "How far away IS this place?"

"About a 45 minute drive" I replied.

"That's a long way to go for DINNER! It better be worth it!" proclaimed Edith.

"I'm just driving. I can't guarantee how good the food will be." I said through clenched teeth.

Edith must have asked me how far away Stacy's was 10 times on this drive...or at least it seemed that way.

"That's a long way to go for DINNER! It better be worth it!"

And about halfway to Heath she turns towards me

225

and shouts, "I FORGOT MY TEETH!! I forgot MY TEETH!!"

As patiently as I could, I told her there was no going back...not for teeth...not for anything.

"Well...it better be GOOD then! They better have soft stuff I can eat!"

This is when I thought about my own Aunt Edith.

After a couple missed turns I finally pulled Big Red into Stacy's parking lot at a little after 4 p.m. Stan's bus was nowhere in sight. My three senior passengers filed into the buffet while I parked Big Red. The rain was beginning to turn to sleet...not frozen yet...but certainly cause for concern. I had never driven this van before and was not interested in snow, sleet or freezing rain on my maiden voyage.

I strolled into Stacy's and the hostess immediately gave me an earful about "that woman over there" lipping off to her and being a general pain in the ass. It seems Edith couldn't decide where she wanted to sit and then complained when no one wanted to sit with her. I sure didn't.

I said to the frustrated hostess, "HEY! Don't bitch to me about her. I just sat next to her for the past hour and have to take her back home!"

When I went to pay for my dinner (you paid up front since it was cafeteria style) she gave me a *senior discount.* And that made me feel a LOT better about things. Now I'm not *just* the driver...I'm one of THEM!

The restaurant was surprisingly busy for "The Early Bird's Early Bird Special". I sat with Don, ate my giant iceberg lettuce salad with the Kraft French Dressing, while we moaned about the return trip with Edith. I ate salad because this place was a fried food lover's utopia. I think the green jello with carrot shavings was deep-fried...maybe even the chairs.

"At least Edna is quiet" I offered to Don.

""Maybe she's just waiting to explode" is what he speculated.

Before I was half finished with my food I see Edith sitting by the front door arguing with the hostess. She has her coat on. She then shouted across the room to me, "I AM DONE! Let's GO! I couldn't eat hardly NOTHIN' 'cause I got no TEETH!"

Don, Edna and I were all still eating. And Stan's bus still wasn't there. I yelled back that we'd be leaving soon...just to try to shut Edith up. Fortunately just then seniors from Stan's bus began trickling into the buffet. And each and every one of them got an update on Edith's plight....both from Edith *and* the hostess...two distinctly different versions of course. If the hostess's eyes had rolled back into her head any further she might have been taken for dead.

Soon enough...but not soon enough for Edith...we

were loading back into Big Red. Much to my dismay Don was standing next to the side door, again sucking down a cig like there was no tomorrow. Smoke began wafting into the van. And as Edith pulled herself into the front passenger seat she began ripping Don a new one.

"I TOLD YOU!! I can't stand SMOKE! Now you're gonna have to take me to the HOSPITAL! You are being STUPID!!"

I asked Don to please stomp out his smoke and get into the van...which he did. Edna sat stone silent. I told Edith we could drive with the windows open until the smoke dissipated. She wasn't buying it.

"I TOLD YOU! I TOLD YOU! I'm putting my MASK on!

Edith pulled out a mask and put it over her face. I sat staring straight ahead...fingers dug into the steering wheel...teeth clenched...pointing Big Red through the sleet on the freeway. And we literally drove for 15 minutes in the cold...and the sleet...with the windows wide open. Don fidgeted in the back. Edna seemed dangerously quiet.

I spat out, "The smoke is gone now Edith" and closed the windows. For a minute or two she seemed to accept this. Then, all too soon she blurted "Do you have any IDEA how HOT IT IS UNDER this MASK?!"

I stared straight ahead...hands tightly on the

wheel...biting my lip.

"No I do not Edith"."

"Well it's HOT! HOT! HOT under a mask like this!!"

""Then take it off." I suggested as politely as I could muster.

To my amazement Edith did just that. And for a brief moment...a very...very brief moment...I thought maybe she might fall asleep...or at least calm down.

Until...

"THAT was a LONG WAY TO GO for DINNER! And it wasn't THAT GOOD EITHER if you ask me!"

It took all the strength in my being not to tell her no one had asked.

Edith continued, "And I asked the waitress for some *tender* chicken tenders but did she bring me *tender* chicken tenders? NO! They were CRUNCHY! I couldn't eat them! All I had was mashed potatoes and gravy 'cause I got no TEETH!!"

The rest of us sat in awe of Edith's mastery of bitching. At least Don and I did. I have no idea what was going through Edna's mind. I again thought of my Aunt Edith.

Perhaps on 4 more occasions we heard "THAT was a LONG WAY TO GO for DINNER! And it wasn't THAT GOOD EITHER if you ask me!"

I was obsessed with getting people home and decided to reward Edna and Don for their patience by dropping them off *before* Edith. But before I could do that Edith had a new mantra...reading the distance signs...which ironically was a bit comforting to me driving a strange vehicle in foul weather.

"30 miles to Columbus" Edith would announce.

"Columbus 19 miles" she'd inform.

"Only 5 miles to Columbus!"

By now it was almost 8 p.m. and dark. Finally...and I mean FINALLY...I got Edna and Don home. Edith calmed down a little after that. I really did understand her anguish about Don's smoking. Still, I did NOT need to hear how it was too far to go for dinner and it wasn't worth it if you asked her...3 more times.

So I pulled Big Red as close to Edith's apartment as I could. The sleet had subsided a little. I helped her out of the van and handed her the walker. I watched as she slowly made her way towards her door...a little stooped but determined...a cantankerous case of dynamite old lady. But...when she got about two thirds of the way to her home...Edith turned toward me...and with a wide toothless smile said, "Thanks Hon! It was a *wonderful evening*!"

Epilogue: People are complex sometimes...especially seniors. There is always something new to learn...whether it's a good thing or not...whether you want to learn or not. A couple days later Edna and Edith got into a conflict on a long trip...almost to Cincinnati. (Hopefully...for all the passengers' sake...it was *good* because that IS a long way to go for lunch!) Apparently on the drive down Edith sat next to Edna and asked her to "move your big purse. I don't have enough room." Edna refused. And for some unknown reason they again sat beside each other for the ride home. And again Edith asked Edna to move her big purse. Edna responded by punching Edith right in the face. Stan had to stop the bus and separate them. So, I guess Don was right. Edna was going to explode. It just took her a while.

Acknowledgments

The website Naked Sunfish began as a 50th birthday present from my lifelong friend Dan Eley. Before its inception I had been asked to write for Crapshoot, a web page by another lifelong bud, Ted Kane. Back then I wasn't sure I *could* write. But Mr. Kane assured me, although all he based his opinion on was my "creative email messages", that I indeed had a knack. And when Dan gave me Naked Sunfish I was unsure I could keep coming up with new material. Yet the three of us have worked together almost nine years now.

So it is with my deepest gratitude that I say thank you to webmaster Dan Eley and featured writer Ted Kane for their faith in me, their loyalty as friends and co-creators, as well as their continued support and commitment. I most certainly hope our "Spontaneous and Sporadic" collaboration will flourish for years to come.

I also want to thank avant-garde poet Dr. John Bennett and artist C. Mehrl Bennett for their constant involvement with Naked Sunfish and guidance with the creative process. Your steadfast dependability and joy of all things possible is always inspirational.

Thanks to those who have been with the "Fish Family" for years: Patrick O'Malley, cyndi o'leary, Jessy Kendell and Alexi Vontsolos. Kudos as well to the relative newcomers: Dennis Toth, Elisa Phillips, Morris Jackson, Sue Alcott, Shawn Gaines and Mark Balsom. Freelancers who have been frequent contributors include: Amelia Hapsari, Wes Boomgaarden, Tara Seibel (with Harvey Pekar), Harry Campbell, Jim Eaton, Anita Branin, Cory Tressler, Emily Glenn, Amy McCrory, Donna Distel, David Hochman, Roberto Lynch, Jonah Baldwin, Rebecca Jewett, Amanda Gradisek, Laura Joseph, Karl Gruber and others too numerous to name.

A very special thank you to all who have proofed my work over the years, some already named. In particular, thanks to Joan Wells for being such a huge help editing this book, for being a fan and friend.

In particular I must single out Ms. Yvonne Brown. I am immensely grateful for her patience, editing skills, companionship and enduring love. Oh yeah....kudos also for her smile, laughter and honesty. To Yvonne, I send a very warm and appreciative thank you, thank you, thank you! For everything.

In closing I must also send out a cosmic thank you to my freshman college English teacher, Mrs. Hathaway...wherever you might be. Okay, so at the ripe old age of 18, I thought writing a journal and have a teacher read it was...well...incredibly stupid. But in reality it was my journal entries that were monumentally stupid. Mrs. Hathaway started me on a path of keeping a journal for almost 16 years. Thank you. I'm sure this is where I learned to put words together. So Thanks Mrs. Hathaway.

Rick Brown

LaVergne, TN USA
07 December 2010
207636LV00008B/4/P

CHAPTER 1
Compassion Fatigue
and Educators

ᴗ𝑝

Baron-Cohen (2011), in his book, *The Science of Evil* devised a scale to measure the capacity of emotional empathy. This scale, referred to as the Empathy Quotient, consists of forty items measuring two key components of empathy. First is the recognition of empathy and second, the response to it. Two versions of this scale have been developed subsequently; a self-report adult version and a child version, completed by a clinical observer. The human psyche is composed of the mind, soul, and spirit and is the central thought, feelings, and motivation, consciously or unconsciously directing the body's reaction to its social and physical environment (Soukhanov, 1984). Over time with situations and circumstances, this full cup of emotional empathy begins to drain and can result in compassion fatigue and eventual burnout of the psyche. Professionals can adapt to change and carry on with their practice, while others ignore these negative changes. Both scenarios consume psychic energy, wearing the professional down. Baron-Cohen describes the vessels of empathy on a spectrum from high to low. At the high end of the spectrum, the vessel of empathy is full.

Conversely, at the low end of the spectrum, the vessel is empty. Baron-Cohen lists ten items of how the vessel can be slowly eroded but alludes to the fact that there are more than ten factors

ᴗ𝑝

impacting empathy at any given time. Baron-Cohen does insert a caveat in the spectrum in that there is a zero-negative and a zero-positive point. Zero-negative points are those individuals identifiable as sociopaths and psychopaths. Zero-positive are individuals on the Autism Spectrum who have zero cognitive ability to recognize empathy situations.

Burnout is a chronic state of exhaustion due to longer-term inter- and intra-personal stress within human services professions (Briere, 2012; Chirkowska-Smolak & Kleka, 2011; Craig & Sprang, 2010; Maslach, Schaufeli & Leiter, 2001; Randler, Luffer & Muller, 2015; Schwarzer & Hallum, 2008; Sprang, Clark & Whitt-Woosley, 2007). Burnout is defined as emotional exhaustion, depersonalization, and reduced accomplishments. Emotional exhaustion refers to feelings of being emotionally overextended and depleted of one's emotional resources, resulting in fatigue, debilitation, loss of energy, and a worn-out feeling. Depersonalization is negative and inappropriate attitudes such as cynicism or irritability, a negative, callous or excessively detached response to other professionals and/or clients, and the loss of idealism (Chirkowska-Smolak & Kleka, 2011; Hoglund, Kringle & Hosan, 2015; Maslach, et al., 2001; Oakes, Lane, Jenkins & Booker, 2013; Oberle & Schonert-Reichl, 2016; Pickering, n.d.; Roeser et al., 2013; Schwarzer & Hallum, 2008). Reduced personal accomplishments refer to how one perceives oneself. It is the self-evaluation component of the psyche and is equated with reduced professional efficacy, productivity or capability, low morale, and the inability to cope with job demands. It is described as a decline in one's feeling of competence and achievement at work. These inadequate coping mechanisms lead to emotional exhaustion and a downward spiral dragging an individual down into an abyss of anxiety, doubt, depression, burnout, and even suicidal ideation.

Adam, Figley, and Boscarino (2008), also recognize compassion fatigue (CF) as a caregiver's reduced capacity or interest in being empathetic or "bearing the suffering of the client, and as the consequential behaviour and emotions resulting from knowing about a traumatizing event experienced or suffered by a person" (p. 3). Part of the diagnostic challenge of this phenomenon is that it is referred to by many names and terms. Listed in Russell and Brickwell (2015) are phrases used to describe the phenomenon throughout history. One such term coined after World War I was, "fight or flight." Another term used in early diagnosis was "voodoo death." This term as described by Russell and Brickwell was found in primitive cultures; also, the term "death by fright" has been used in more modern societies. Russell and Brickwell describe modern societies from the time period of WWII onwards, where the term "general adaptive syndrome" was used to describe idiopathic seizures. This term attempted to describe medically unexplained physical conditions often associated with stress-related injuries.

General adaptive syndrome was a phrase coined in post-World War II research, to consist of alarm, resistance, and eventual exhaustion. In more recent times, the terms *professional burnout, secondary traumatic stress, vicarious traumatization, empathy distress fatigue, occupational stress injury* (OSI), and *compassion stress injury* (CSI) are used interchangeably. CF is still very broad and does not adequately describe symptomology. Symptomology is the set of symptoms characteristic of a medical condition or exhibited by a patient necessary for a diagnosis. I prefer the description; *empathy-erosion* of the psyche, because the term erosion infers that it is constantly occurring and can be caused by an immediate event or gradually over a period of time. I will strive to use the term CSI, tying the other terminology in with how and why it causes stress-induced injury and describing how it impacts professionals. The purpose for clarifying the terminology is to allow readers and therapists the ability to articulate the injury when documenting and reporting. The purpose of my study is to examine CSI in teachers at all levels of the education spectrum.

CHAPTER 2
Historically the Cups of Empathy

The following includes approximately forty articles and two books, all dealing with the theme of compassion fatigue CF. The itself is loosely divided into eight sections, each dealing with a different aspect of CF. The first section is an overview of CF, its causes, terminology, and definitions and of the risk of developing CF. The second section defines what lack of empathy is and how it can be scaled. The third section focuses on therapy approaches. This section is further divided into the linkages between psychological, social, behavioral, and physical symptoms as well as neurological indicators of CF. These linkages are also associated to post-traumatic stress disorder (PTSD), anxiety disorders, attachment theory, and its potential basis for CF. This section also looks at how mindfulness training has been potentially linked to compassion renewal, and finally, how using neurological imagining, compassion, and empathy are linked and how the lack of compassion or the eroding of empathy has been termed an identifiable psychological condition referred to as Compassion Stress Injury CSI or Occupational Stress Injury OSI.

The fourth and fifth sections link the methodology of identifying CF using various tools and scales that have been developed. There is a discussion in the literature of what forms and direction research should be taken to further investigate markers of

CF and what supports need to be identified, strengthened, and implemented to assist individuals who fall into the CSI category. The last section addresses the connection I found myself making between my personal experiences as an educator and CF.

Each of the articles reviewed for this paper define CF. Although there were forty different explanations of CF, each article had four or five foundational characteristics or themes that identify CF.

A sample of these terms used in the literature review include *empathy erosion* (Elangovan, Auer-Rizzi & Szabo, 2015; Lee, et al., 2014; O'Brien & Haaga, 2015; Oberle & Schonert-Reichl, 2016; Russell & Brickell, 2015; Zeidner, Hadar, Matthews, & Roberts, 2013), *burnout* (Lee, et al., 2014; Merriman, 2015; O'Brien & Haaga, 2015; Oberle & Schonert-Reichl, 2016; Pfifferling & Gilley, 2000; Pickering, n.d.; Skaalvik & Skaalvik, 2016; Sprang, et al., 2007; Zeidner et al., 2013), *vicarious trauma* (Babble, 2012; Merriman, 2015; O'Brien & Haaga, 2015; Russell & Brickell, 2015; Sprang, et al., 2007; Zeidner et al., 2013), *secondary traumatic stress disorder* (Merriman, 2015; O'Brien & Haaga, 2015; Sprang, et al., 2007; Zeidner et al., 2013), *anxiety disorder* (Lee, et al., 2014; Russell & Brickell, 2015; Zeidner et al., 2013), and PTSD (Briere, 2012; Merriman, 2015; O'Brien & Haaga, 2015; Russell & Brickell, 2015).

The first theme is that all articles in the review identified that CF is, in all its forms, a deep physical, emotional, and spiritual exhaustion accompanied by acute emotional pain (Pfifferling & Gillery, 2000), wherein an individual is unable to refuel and regenerate compassion and empathy; this, in turn, leads to cynicism and inefficacy (Maslach et al., 2001).

The second common theme among the articles were symptoms described as a wide range of psychological issues such as dissociation, anger, anxiety, and sleep disturbances such as nightmares, to a feeling of powerlessness (Babble, 2012).

Third common ground was that physical symptoms range from nausea, headache, general constriction of body function, bodily temperature change, dizziness, fainting spells, and impaired hearing (Babble, 2012).

A fourth theme or cornerstone is that CF is caused by some form of trauma (Briere, 2012). This trauma can be instantaneous, such as a natural or man-made catastrophic event (Randler et al., 2015), or the trauma can be a slow-moving series of events that takes place over time (Bhutani, Bhutani, Balhara, & Kalra, 2012; Briere, 2012; Craig & Sprang, 2010; Negash & Sahin, 2011), literally eroding an individual's level of empathy, compassion, and trust (Briere, 2012; Elangovan, et al., 2015; Lee, et al., 2015).

CF is not reserved for white, middle-class, heterosexual members of society but is an international, cross-cultural, multi-societal phenomenon in various professions (Chirkowska- Smolak & Kleka, 2011; Hakanen et al., 2006) that has been studied from the late 1950s through the '60s, when the term "burnout" was first used, and then recognized as a significant phenomenon of the modern age (Maslach, et al., 2001). It is now identified as extreme fatigue and loss of idealism and passion for one's job (Briere, 2012; Chirkowska-Smolak & Kleka, 2011; Craig, & Sprang, 2010; Maslach et al., 2001; Randler et al., 2015; Sprang et al., 2007). It took considerable time for burnout to become recognized in professional circles, and this proceeded through several phases. Maslach (1976) and Freudenberger (1975) have been credited with moving the concept of burnout into mainstream professional discourse.

While reviewing the literature, it became quickly evident that a fifth common theme emerged for CF, which as well as being a global phenomenon, is not restricted to one particular field or occupation. Although the human services are more prevalent in the literature, other fields are also present, including *health care workers; physicians* (Adams et al., 2008; Bhutani et al., 2012; Gleichgerrecht & Decety, 2013; Pfifferling & Gilley, 2000; Zeidner et al., 2013), *nurses* (Adams et al., 2008; Bhutani et al., 2012; Mason & Nel, 2012; Zeidner et al., 2013), *therapists of*

7

all kinds (Beaumont, Durkin, Hollins-Martin, & Carson, 2015; Berzoff & Kita, 2010; Briere, 2012; Craig & Sprang, 2010; Lee, et al., 2015; Llewellyn, 2009; Merriman, 2015; Negash & Sahin, 2011; O'Brien & Haaga, 2015; Russell & Brickell, 2015; Sprang, et al., 2007), or any service that is in direct contact with another human, such as *teachers* (Froese-Germain, 2014; Hakanen et al., 2006; Hoglund et al., 2015; Kyriacou, 2001; McGuire, 1981; Oakes, et al., 2013; Oberle & Schonert-Reichl, 2016; Pickering, n.d.; Roeser, et al., 2013; Schwarzer & Hallum, 2008; Skaalvik & Skaalvik, 2016; Skinner & Beers, n.d.), *social workers* (Randler et al., 2015) and *first responders*, like emergency medical technicians (EMT), firefighter, ambulance attendant, or law enforcement officials (Chirkowska-Smolak & Kleka, 2011; Elangovan et al., 2015; Maslach et al., 2001; O'Brien & Haaga 2015; Pardess, Mikulincer, Dekel & Shaver, 2013; Randler et al., 2015), whether volunteers or in paid positions.

Adam et al. (2008) have documented that over the past twenty-plus years, most research has focused on psychosocial stressors on individuals seeking social support and coping assistance after a negative or traumatic event. However, relatively little research has focused on the formal caregivers and their well-being and social support when providing needed services to traumatized clients. These professionals are most likely to be secondarily exposed to the traumatic event, and over time they develop into the diagnostic criteria of PTSD or vicarious trauma. This has been termed the "double-edge sword" of human empathy by Russell and Brickell (2015), in which transference and counter-transference occurs between patient and client (Berzoff & Kita, 2010; Elangovan et al., 2015; Russell & Brickell, 2015). Transference is a psychological term that refers to a client transferring his/her issues or situations over to or onto the therapist's emotional psyche. Cormier, Nurius, and Osborn (2013) describe this transfer as positive, negative, or mixed. A positive transference can strengthen the relationship, wherein the therapist provides missing elements of understanding, impartiality, and reliability.

A negative transference or counter transference is when the feelings, thoughts, values, and beliefs of the therapist begin to influence the therapeutic relationship. Counter transference in Cormier, et al., (2013) can have unwanted negative consequences, which can potentially led to unethical practices or conduct by the therapist. A therapist must always be aware of physical sensations, emotional cues, and psychological manifestations of values and beliefs that encroach upon the therapeutic relationship. It is normal for human beings to have thoughts and feelings about clients and treatment provided. But what is required within any therapeutic relationship is the ethical adherence to preventing those thoughts and feelings from negatively impacting the therapeutic progress.

Three articles drew specific attention to CF based on an erosion of empathy, which has been termed empathic accuracy and the subsequent trust factor. The first article by O'Brien and Haaga (2015) looked at empathic accuracy and CF amongst therapists in training and how exposure to intense negative emotions and experiences presented by patients can take a psychological toll on therapists and in the worst case, result in potential burnout, or CF, also known as vicarious trauma. They differentiate the three terms, identifying specific characteristics associated with each. Burnout is characterized by emotional exhaustion in the wake of long-term exposure to frustration and stressful aspects of one's work. CF can occur after a single therapy session. Vicarious trauma is more a descriptive of change occurring in the therapist's schemata about the therapist and the world after hearing about trauma from clients. Due to the shift in a therapist's schemata, the full value of his or her empathy becomes eroded. O'Brien and Haaga refer to this as emotional affect, where the extent of a person's ability to comprehend (empathize with) what someone else is thinking, feeling, and expressing becomes compromised.

Emotional affect is a gradual erosion of the full cup of empathy that is brought to the classroom or treatment facility. It is nefarious because the erosion occurs without any cognitive awareness of the professional. "The taxing nature of the work conducted by [professionals] may lead to... mental health effects... and, in the most extreme cases, cause [professionals] to drop out from [their] field as a result of burnout or CF." (O'Brien & Haaga, 2015, p. 5)

Lee, et al., (2015) support the above, but go on to explicitly identify counselor empathy as the ability to understand a patient's experience and share that understanding, and it is seen as an integral component of the relationship. From this basis, the authors, Lee et al., identify markers relevant to all professions in an attempt to identify who and what professions might be most prone to CF. They list triggers of CF, such as delivering bad news or an inability to prevent suffering. They listed some personality traits such as wanting to be in control, wanting to be acknowledged, tending towards perfectionism, being self-critical, and facing a greater difficulty managing stressful events. One key factor identified as a risk factor for CF was anxiety. Anxiety, defined by Lee et al., is a natural human reaction to unpleasant or threatening stimuli. It includes physiological, emotional, and cognitive responses and can be further subdivided into state anxiety and trait anxiety. State anxiety is when the subjective feeling of tension, apprehension, nervousness, and worry occurs at any given moment. Trait anxiety is individual differences in relation to situations or the difference in the intensity and frequency, based on the individual's ability to cope with anxiety from past experiences. Higher trait anxiety individuals perceive situations as more stressful and threatening, and they experience a more intense increase in their anxiety level. To control this higher anxiety level, they become hyper-vigilant by being overly cautious to maintain control of situations, to protect themselves from uncontrolled situations, and to avoid dissatisfaction about themselves as professionals.

A theme that occurs in the literature is how empathy by the professional is eroded over time and how this erosion undermines the trust between customer and salesperson; patient and doctors, nurse, or therapist; student and teacher; teacher and administration. The focus then becomes how to repair the breach of trust so that both parties may move forward, either together or separately. Elangovan et al. (2015) suggest four conditions that erode care and break down the trust factor. First of the conditions is some form of psychological contract violation; second, a breakdown or a betrayal of trust, which could be distrust of a person, scenario, setting, or situation; and third is revenge. Fourth is that erosion of trust is a result of two distinct steps; a violation of trust or an event. A violation of trust can trigger and prompt the truster to assess the situation on an emotional as well as cognitive level. Emotionally, there could be anger, hurt, fear, and frustration that the trust has been violated. Cognitively, the truster will engage in what Kahneman (2013) calls System 2 Thinking: slow thought and thinking processes when the truster re-thinks the value, validity or reliability of the relationship with individual he/she trusts.

While the topic of CF covers a wide range of professions and terminology, a distinct effort was made to narrow the focus down to the occupation of professional educators.

Professionals in any occupation very seldom practice their professions in a vacuum, and anxiety is not new to the human condition. But what is new is how within a professional's practice, whether that be as a therapist or an educator, the interaction between humans can have either a positive or negative effect. The third article by Oberle and Schonert-Reichl (2016) looks at how stress within a classroom of a teacher high on the trait and state anxiety continuum has adverse effects on the students' morning cortisol levels were then linked to a teacher's occupational stress to students' physiological stress regulators. This phenomenon is referred to as the *personality-stress contagion theory*, in which stressful experiences can spill over from one stressed individual to another within a shared social setting. The use of salivary cortisol levels as an indicator of stress is based on the physiological fact that stress reactivity can be accessed via the reactivity of the hypothalamic-pituitary-adrenal (HPA) axis, which is a homeostatic system that follows a circadian rhythm and is activated in response to cognitive stimulation or stressors. In a normal situation, the cortisol levels peak within twenty to forty-give minutes after waking and then gradually decline. A flat slope or no indication of a downward trend throughout the day suggests a dysregulation of the axis due to certain variables. However an upwards slope indicates activation of cortisol due to stress occurring throughout the work day, associated to state-anxiety, these can be indicators of mental health problems in children and adults or indicators of metabolic, immune, or nervous system issues from the prolonged exposure to stress. In this article, they measure the stress of a teacher experiencing burnout, emotional erosion, or CF.

Teaching is a unique profession. Educators are always finding themselves under the microscope of a societal lens, being on the front line of changes, good or bad, that occur in an ever-changing world. In my experience, most teachers would like to be left alone to do the job they have been trained to do: teach children. But they are constantly interrupted, challenged, or required to change based on circumstances and decisions made beyond their scope or circle of influence, thereby creating stress in the teacher and in the school environment. This is not a new phenomenon. In 1981, McGuire wrote an essay that points out that teachers' self-esteem is constantly being challenged by external as well as internal forces (Edinger, Houts, Meyer & Sand, 1981). Teachers have been instructed by bureaucratics and top down administrators, according to McGuire, toward greater productivity, leading teachers to experience job related stress, burnout, and dropout from the profession entirely. In an effort to prevent the aforementioned conditions, McGuire lists eight steps that should be implemented in an attempt to improve the teaching profession. First, improve teacher education so it more nearly reflects the world of practice and as a result the new teacher can thrive in a school setting. Second, consider the impact that legislation has upon the education profession. Legislators intending to do good by their constituents are constantly mandating more and more programs for teachers to implement. However, this increases the burden upon the educational setting, which is already overloaded with school programming and staff development necessary to implement said programming. The third recommendation by McGuire is to increase teacher decision-making powers. By giving teachers more autonomy for what, how, when, and what resources to utilize, it is hoped that this degree of control can alleviate some of the pent-up stress teachers are encountering on a daily basis. The fourth recommendation is to improve administrative supports. This entails new efforts to be more supportive of teaching staff by providing a more secure environment in the hope that teachers can expend more of their professional energy teaching and supporting students. McGuire's fifth strategy is to employ a drastic decrease in class size, which he suggests would allow more individualized instruction and more extensive counseling of students, thereby eradicating violence and vandalism occurring at and in the schools. The sixth strategy suggested is that public education must be given the financial priority necessary to make the fullest use of educational resources. In theory, this would eliminate overcrowded classrooms, provide appropriate education for students of special needs, and encourage the gifts and talents of students. It also would allow an upgrade in instructional material allowing teachers adequate preparation time, and offer teachers sabbaticals and other opportunities to reflect upon their work and develop professional acumen. The seventh strategy suggested is to increase public awareness and information in regards to teachers' workload. Finally, he recommends acting upon short-term remedies, collectively, by planning and implementing procedures that will either prevent teacher stress and burnout before they occur or deal with them immediately should they occur.

Six years after McGuire's (1981) work was published: educators' multitudes of working responsibilities had not changed. Russell et al. (1987) wrote that education is a particularly stressful occupation with many negative aspects such as disciplinary problems, student apathy, overcrowded classrooms, involuntary (staff) transfers, excessive paperwork, inadequate salaries, demanding or unsupportive parents, and lack of administrative support. This results in teachers experiencing burnout manifested as physical and psychological symptoms and resulting in teacher attrition. Russell et al. report that studies of the causes for teacher burnout indicated that age, sex, and grade level taught were significant predictors of the Maslach Burnout Inventory (MBI). Russell et al. reported from the MBI, that; younger or novice teachers reported greater emotional exhaustion; that negative attitudes towards students, referred to as depersonalization, was reported by male teachers in general, and secondary teachers specifically. What Russell et al., does describe is that a greater sense of accomplishment was reported by elementary school teachers in general. The reason postulated for this greater sense of accomplishment, or compassion renewal, was social support from colleagues, administrative support, and finally parental support. Russell et al. used a tool called the Social Provisions Scale (SPS), which was designed to measure a person's current social relationship based on six relational provisions described by a researcher called Weiss (1974). These provisions are attachment, solid integration, reassurance of worth, guidance from a trust-worthy authority figure, reliable alliances amongst peers, and finally, an opportunity for nurturance where a person is responsible for the well-being of another.

Emotional exhaustion was reported by younger teachers, and more negative attitudes towards students, referred to as depersonalization, was reported by male and secondary teachers. (Froese-Germain, 2014; Russell et al., 1987; Skaalvik & Skaalvik, 2016)

On a positive note, a greater sense of personal accomplishment was reported by elementary school teachers. The authors investigated what strategies could be implemented to prevent teacher burnout. They determined that individuals with high levels of social support were in better physical and psychological health, suggesting that increasing social support for teachers may be a useful strategy for preventing teacher burnout. The authors were curious about exactly what form of social support could assist teachers. Their participants completed the SPS.

The MBI (Maslach et al., 2001) was originally designed for use in the human services occupation and in health care in 1981. A second version was developed for use by people working in educational settings, termed the MBI-Educational Survey (MBI-ES). These inventories assess burnout via three dimensions: *emotional exhaustion, depersonalization, and reduced personal accomplishments*. A third version for general use in professions has been developed, called the MBI-General Survey (MBI-GS) and identifies *exhaustion, cynicism, and reduced professional efficacy*. The MBI tools are considered statistically valid and reliable and have been adopted across cultures to be acceptable measurable standards (Chirkowski-Smolak & Kleka, 2011; Hakanen et al., 2006; Russell et al., 1987).

SPS is a tool designed to assess the extent to which a person's current social relationship includes six relational provisions: attachment, social integration, reassurance of worth, guidance, reliable alliance, and opportunity for maintenance. SPS developers determined that a lack of three particular aspects of social support was found to be a prediction of burnout: lack of support from one's supervisor(s); lack of reassurance of worth: and lack of reliable alliances amongst peers.

As reported earlier, occupational stress is not culturally unique—it is found in all professional formats and is a worldwide phenomenon. Hakanen et al. (2006) studied the connections between burnout and work engagement among teachers. Part of their evidence came from a study in Finland, where educators were experiencing higher levels of burnout compared to workers in other human services and jobs.

Burnout is a combination of symptoms of exhaustion, physical, psychological, and spiritual, resulting in cynicism and reduced professional efficacy. Exhaustion refers to feeling of strain, particularly chronic fatigue from an overtaxing workload. Cynicism is an indifference or distant attitude towards work in general, the people with whom one works, and a feeling that work has lost its meaning. Lack of professional efficacy is a reduced feeling of competence, achievement, and accomplishment in one's job and the organization.

Hakanen et al. (2006) describe work engagement as a positive, fulfilling, work-related state of mind characterized by vigor, dedication, and absorption.

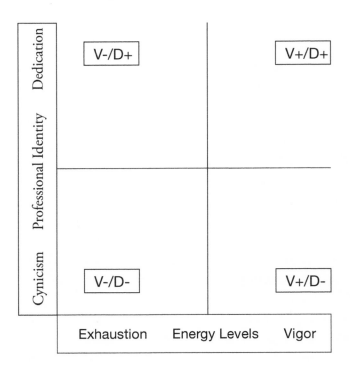

Figure 1 Professional identity and energy quadrants

Vigor is having high levels of energy and mental resilience. Dedication is a sense of significance, enthusiasm, inspiration, pride, and challenge. Absorption is being fully concentrated and engrossed in one's work effort. These create in one's mind a four-quadrant diagram of two continuums intersecting at midpoint, identified as a professional. The horizontal axis is energy with exhaustion at the negative and vigor at the positive. The vertical axis is professional identity with dedication at the positive end and cynicism at the negative end. New professionals would be situated in the top-right quadrant of high dedication and high vigor. Those experiencing factors that are impacting their performance and energy could potentially find themselves in the lower left-hand quadrant with negative energy and negative identification, manifested as cynicism. According to this model, excessive work engagement results in a process of wearing out employees' mental and physical resources and may, therefore, lead to burnout and eventually ill health, physically and psychologically. Energetic process occurs from high job demands, where employees under stress face a trade-off between protection of their primary performance goals (a salary) and the mental effort required to be invested in their job. As job demands increase, regulator problems occur. In other words, compensation demands do not keep pace with increased demands to maintain performance level, resulting in physiological and psychological costs. To break this cycle, Hakanen et al. (2006) refer to motivational process, which links job resources with organizational commitment through work engagement. Job resources are viewed as an intrinsically motivational tool, which fosters employees' growth, learning, and development, or, extrinsically, as a means to achieve work goals. From a social context, intrinsic motivation satisfies basic human needs of autonomy, competence, and relatedness and increases well-being and commitment. By satisfying basic needs, the outcome for the professional is positive and fulfilling, resulting in commitment to the organization.

Hakanen et al. (2006) uses a job demands-resources model (JD-RM) for their study to show that emotional demands due to pupil misbehavior and work overload can be important predictors of job stress. A JD-RM is a tool used to identify what strain or job stress is causing a disturbance in the balance between job demand and resources available to complete the job.

Job demands refer to those physical, psychological, social, or organizational aspects of the job that require a sustained physical and psychological effort and result in certain physiological and psychological costs. These job demands become stressors in situations where high effort is required to sustain an expected performance level, such as managing disruptive pupil behaviour, work overload, and a poor physical work environment (Hakanen et al., 2006, p. 497). Job resources refer to those physical, social, psychological, or organizational aspects of the job that may reduce job demands and are associated with reduced physiological and psychological costs, resulting in achieving work goals and stimulating personal growth, learning, and development; thereby renewing emotional energy (Hakanen et al., 2006, p. 497). Five job resources have been identified: job control, access to information, supervisory support, innovative school climate, and social climate (Hakanen et al., 2006, p. 497). Job control is the ability to make autonomous decisions directly impacting the responsibilities of the position held; access to information is where pertinent material is readily available to allow progress to proceed within the organization to reach objectives; and supervisory support is where the supervisor supports the employee without prejudice or bias in decisions the employee makes without fear of ridicule or punishment. An innovative school climate (Hakanen et al., 2006, p. 499) is one where staff is encouraged to be innovative in educating their students, objectively, without fear of retribution or chastising, subjectively, by others or administration (Hakanen et al., 2006, p. 498). As well, decisions affecting the whole school are openly discussed, debated, and mutually decided upon; rather than a top-down, authoritative decision-making approach, which Hakanen et al. (2006, p. 496), describe as the demands-control model (DCM). A social climate (Hakanen et al., 2006, p. 498) is built on trust and is one where collegial support is freely reciprocated. Hakanen et al., define burnout, exhaustion, and cynicism as a result of what can happen in schools, which is in contrast to the professional efficacy, work engagement, and energetic process that is desired.

Schwarzer and Hallum (2008) studied perceived teacher self-efficacy between Syrian and German educators as a predictor of job stress and burnout, using a meta-analysis. This is an analysis of data from multiple studies searching for common indicators of strength to support concepts. The concepts proposed were that teacher engagement is positively associated with personal coping resources, whereas teacher burnout is indicated by a number of negative personality characteristics, including low levels of self-efficacy. In this study, using evidence from Bandura's (1997) work, Schwarzer and Hallum proposed that self-efficacy can either enhance or impede motivation. The suggestion is that people with high levels of self-efficacy choose to perform more challenging tasks; as well as, set higher goals for themselves and stick to them. Actions are shaped by the thinking process and people are able to anticipate either optimistic or pessimistic scenarios based on their self-efficacy. Schwarzer and Hallum suggest that individuals with high self-efficacy invest more time and effort and persist longer than those with lower levels of self-efficacy. This was supported by the use of a tool developed by Schwarzer & Jerusalem (1995) called the General Self-Efficacy (GSE) scale. The researchers trace the development of efficacy back to Bowlby's attachment theory, where individuals with high levels of efficacy probably had secure attachment, while those with lower levels of efficacy may have had some form of insecure attachment. Their study was divided into two: Study I of 1203 participants, and Study II, which was a longitudinal study of 458 teachers. Study I found that younger teachers and those with low general self-efficacy either left the profession or went on medical leaves more often. In Study II, low self-efficacy preceded burnout, but in those incidents where intervention was put into place to strengthen teacher self-efficacy, fewer burnout cases were reported.

Interestingly, this cross-cultural study supported evidence from a 1996 study of Canadian educators (Schwarzer & Hallum, 2008) and a 2000 study of Hong Kong educators (Schwarzer & Hallum, 2008), which are studies that measure the cross-cultural aspect of CF and found evidence that psychometric properties are satisfactorily valid and reliable and consistent across cultures. In Froese-Germain (2014) and Schwarzer and Hallum, they support the fact that burnout in educators is an international concern and low self-efficacy of the educator seems to have some significance. This study by Schwarzer and Hallum, describes self-efficacy, which is belief in oneself. This has the ability to enhance or impede motivation. People with high self-efficacy set higher goals and stick to them, perform more challenging tasks, and have actions which are pre-shaped by thoughts. They anticipate being either optimistic or pessimistic dependent upon their level of perceived self-efficacy. Highly self-efficacious people invest effort and time; they persist longer than those with low self-efficacy. They recover more quickly from setbacks and maintain a commitment to their goals. They select challenging settings, explore their environments or create new ones.

The Canadian Teachers' Federation and the Alberta Teachers' Association have recognized the symptomology of stressors in the field of education as trends. These trends show new teachers leaving the profession and experienced teachers remaining but falling into the category of medical leaves as a result of job stress. The Pickering (n.d.) article tries to find a balance between the stress of work and the work of stress. In this article, Pickering highlights that educators across Canada undergo a general adaptive syndrome when coping with psychological and physiological responses to demanding or tense situations and that there is a direct link between the individual and the environment. The individual goes through three stages when in a stressful environment: Stage 1 involves reactions based on the fight or flight component of survival; Stage 2 involves resistance where the body maintains a heightened sense of awareness and continues to fight against the perceived threat; finally, Stage 3, is exhaustion, where the body has run out of energy reserve and an imbalance occurs, which, in turn, results in the body wearing down or burning out.

The National Institute of Occupational Safety and Health of the United States, in 1999, listed six job conditions that may lead to stress and eventual burnout. They are: design of the tasks, managerial style, interpersonal relationships, work roles, career concerns, and environmental conditions. These findings are supported by Froese-Germain (2014), who note that teachers work between ten to twenty hours per week outside of regular school hours, which adds stress and exhaustion and leads to high rates of absenteeism and burnout. As well, teachers' work is highly complex and involves a wide range of tasks. Teachers as a result, often multi-task, which prevents them from focusing on much higher-order activities (Levitin, 2014) such as planning, engaging in professional development, and reflecting on their practice. It is a fact that a modern classroom has a wide range of learning needs and teachers lack the support and resources necessary to support this diverse population. Finally, government-directed bureaucratic mandates, administrative demands, and parent requests, as well as high-stakes testing and accountability factors, increase the amount of precious time teachers spend on paperwork, administrative requirements, formal assessments of students, and reporting, leading to over-taxed, stressed, and anxiety-laden educators. What is still missing from the discussion is the ever-changing curriculum and resource material, which is an effort to keep the teacher and the educational system ahead of the ever-changing world.

Besides the element of burnout, Pickering (n.d.) lists twelve phases of burnout, noting that an individual may find him or herself in more than one stage at a time and that each one has varying lengths of time. These include a pressure to work harder, neglecting personal needs, displacement of conflict, revision of values, denial of emerging problems, withdrawal, obvious behaviour changes, depersonalization, inner emptiness, depression, and finally, total burnout syndrome, which includes both mental and physical collapse (p. 16). Pickering's article analyzes the impact that stress and burnout, have on the educational profession in Canada. The research indicates that this is a national crisis. Educators are ranked second, behind ambulance drivers, for experiencing worse than average physical health or psychological well-being, and sixth in regards to job satisfaction. This evidence is supported by the use of sick leave in a survey conducted by Desjardins Financial (2000, as cited in Pickering, n.d.) and Statistics Canada (2005) respectively. The Desjardins Financial survey highlighted thirty-five million lost workdays a year; (Pickering, n.d.), forty percent of health-related problems are stress and mental health concerns, and there is a forty percent turnover of professionals in the field of education. The survey also reports that sixty percent of Canadian workers will go to work, regardless of their physical or psychological well-being. According to a Statistics Canada survey, teachers and professors are absent 9.3 days a year and these are taken as sick leave. However, for secondary and elementary teachers, the number of days absent is greater than the average, about 10.7 days, and professors are absent on average 6.7 days per year. Administrators across Canada, in 2006, were concerned about the amount of absenteeism occurring in their schools. Quebec led the concern with 35.7 percent of teachers in the study, then Ontario at 18.2 percent, followed by British Columbia at 16.6 percent, the Prairie Provinces with 14.8 percent, and finally, the Atlantic Provinces at 12.3 percent (Pickering, n. d.). A caveat of the Pickering article is that that numbers provided are in percentages, and that the total number of respondents was not recorded.

Since these findings have become evident, different attempts have been made to ward off the causes of stress and to alleviate burnout among educators. Oakes et al. (2013) looked at a three-tiered model of prevention of teacher burnout based on teacher efficacy. It is referred to as the comprehensive, integrated, three-tiered (CI3T) model of prevention. This study, carried out in the USA, tries to draw linkages between a teacher's sense of efficacy and burnout. The study utilizes two middle schools including grades six through eight, located in a southern state. Eighty-six educators with an average of ten years' experience responded to the study. They compared the Teacher's Sense of Efficacy Scale (TSES) with the MBI. The TSES is a twenty-four-item instrument consisting of three moderately correlated subscales: efficacy of student engagement, efficacy of instructional strategies, and efficacy in classroom management. Efficacy is the belief that one can effect change in his or her environment (Oakes et al., 2013). For teachers, efficacy is defined as their own judgment of their capabilities to produce desired outcomes of students learning and engagement (Oakes et al., 2013). In other words, teachers' judgments influence their goals, effort, and persistence with teaching tasks.

Oakes et al. postulate that by establishing a three-tiered model of prevention based on teacher self-efficacy rating, that the educational system would benefit students and result in lower leaves of stress and absences by educators. The model is described as Tier I (for all students), Tier 2 (for some students), and Tier 3 (for a few students) of support and instruction. These tiers are based on evidence such as universal practice and programming; universal screening procedures to detect students who may need additional support; and supports of increasing intensity regarding duration, frequency, specialization instruction, and smaller teacher-student ratio. The tiers then utilize various methods of monitoring student progress toward expected outcomes and benchmarks and finally recommend procedures for assessing program implementation.

In their analysis, Oakes et al. (2013) find that in regards to burnout, the mean and frequency scores indicate a moderate to high level of emotional exhaustion and a high level of personal accomplishment, but a lower mean score of depersonalization. Interestingly, one predictive factor associated with emotional exhaustion is an educator's level of education: The higher the level of education achieved, the higher the depersonalization score. In regards to depersonalization, a negative relationship was discovered between depersonalization scores and treatment integrity score, suggesting that implementing the model as planned has a lower level of depersonalization. Finally, with personal accomplishment, a negative relationship occurs where female teachers report lower levels of personal accomplishment than do their male counterparts.

Attempts have been made to investigate how to lower the rate of burnout. Randler et al. (2015) theorize that the circadian rhythm of adults versus students would have an impact on teacher burnout. They looked at assessing morningness-eveningness in teachers and its relationship to a sense of coherence in occupational requirements and burnout. They utilize the Composite Scale of Morningness (CSM) and Sense of Coherence (SOC) plus the MBI. SOC is defined by Randle et al., as an aspect of well-being and health. It is a way of making sense of the world when a major factor is determining how a person manages stress and stays healthy. It includes three components; comprehensibility, which is the belief that what happens in their lives is rational, predictable, structured, and understandable; manageability, which is adequate and sufficient resources to help manage difficulties as they arise; and, finally, meaningfulness, in that the demands created by exposure to adversity are seen as a challenge and are worthy of engagement.

Morningness-eveningness is the timeframe at which individuals are at their optimum cognitive performance level (Randler et al., 2015). According to this study, morningness in teachers results in lower emotional exhaustion; coherence is high, and personal accomplishment is positive. This suggests that morningness is an influential predictor of teacher well-being. The irony of this study is in its relation to students and their circadian rhythm. Children need a certain number of hours of quality sleep to learn, master, and understand their world (Berger, 2011). A teacher's optimum cognitive timeframe is morningness and student optimum time frame is late afternoon or eveningness. This unparalleled dichotomy is sure to result in conflict, hostility, anxiety, and avoidance-type behaviour by both participants.

This segues into the next article by Hoglund et al. (2015). Although their article focuses on high-needs elementary schools, the unparalleled dichotomy is still relevant. Hoglund et al. looked at classroom risks, resources, and how teacher burnout is tied to classroom quality and children's adjustment to an academic setting. They define high needs as schools with enrollment of low-income and visible minorities in a socially vulnerable neighborhood. In this type of setting, teachers can be overwhelmed by job-related stressors that can elevate feelings of burnout and undermine the quality of classroom instruction.

Teachers experiencing burnout have a difficult time creating a nurturing, high quality, supportive, and organized classroom. Being emotionally exhausted, teachers tend to believe that they are not reaching their professional goals, and many struggle to build supportive, respectful relationships amongst their students and peers. They may also lack sensitivity to support children's learning and may ineffectively re-direct children's behaviour. The study finds that teacher burnout predicts negative growth or erosion, in the teacher-child relationship, and this interacts with external behavior to predict negative changes in children's quality of relationships with teachers and friends, their school engagement, and their literacy skills across the school term. The author describes this situation as a source of double-jeopardy; external behaviour plus a teacher experiencing burnout leads to poorer relationships with teachers and peers as well as poorer school engagement and academic skills.

The next focus of the literature review is that of compassion renewal (CR), and the various therapeutic methodologies used to fully refill the cup of empathy, compassion, and job satisfaction. This section looks at varying degrees of CF or burnout, aligning it with anxiety, PTSD, and as it is now labeled in the therapy world, as CSI or OSI. Skinner and Beer (n.d.) look at the potential technique of mindfulness to assist teachers in coping with stress and to build on teacher resilience. They list two ways that teachers tend to cope, but both are described as maladaptive. They include avoidance and escaping, or emotion-focused coping strategies, such as working harder and longer hours to prove their worth to themselves and supervisors. Both are associated with higher levels of psychological distress, anxiety, somatic complaints, emotional exhaustion, depersonalization, physical symptoms, and burnout and lower levels of personal accomplishment and job satisfaction. The authors suggest that mindfulness could be an intervention method to aid teachers in developing personal resources that would help them cope more constructively with the stress and anxiety of their profession. This constructive kind of coping is to promote engagement and learning and to identify and provide multiple points in the process that would make a difference.

The process involves two appraisals. The first is to evaluate what is at stake for the person in the stressful, anxious-laden encounter. The second is to evaluate the encounter: Is there harm or loss involved? Are either of these sustainable and reversible? Is there a threat anticipated which has not yet occurred? Finally, is there a challenge based on eagerness and excitement involved with the situation? These secondary appraisals allow for rational decision-making processes to occur, enabling a method of control or coping to become established so that a situation can be dealt with effectively. This is what Kahneman (2013) would refer to as System 2 Thinking processes.

From a therapeutic viewpoint, the caregiver must understand the following terms put forth by Briere (2012). Traumatic reaction can be instantaneous or from prolonged exposure. Regardless, both are referred to as psychological trauma, wherein memories are formed and carried forward with emotion, cognition, and sensation that becomes associated with the trauma. These can be triggered and re-lived as flashbacks, intrusive thoughts, painful feelings and other aspects of PTSD.

Trauma can breach our assumption of ourselves, our safety, our future, and even the goodness of people. Trauma can also involve existential confrontation, leaving the affected person feeling alone, irrevocably changed, and flooded with awareness of the fragility of life. Compassion is referred by Briere (2012) from two perspectives. First, from a context of relationship psychotherapy, and secondly from a spiritual or contemplative approach.

Compassion is defined as being non-judgmentally aware and appreciative of the predicament and suffering of others, with a desire to relieve that suffering and increase well-being. It includes a positive emotional state involving feelings of unconditional care, kindness, and warmth. Empathy is the understanding and appreciation of a client's experience and difficulties. Mindfulness is the capacity to sustain moment-by-moment focused awareness of and openness to the client, as well as to the therapist's role, without judgment, providing unconditional acceptance regardless of circumstances, whether they be physical, social, emotional, financial, racial or cultural. Briere's is a Western clinician's viewpoint. He describes three forms of treatment therapy: exposure therapy, cognitive therapy and relational psychotherapy. Exposure and cognitive therapy both include techniques to increase a client's emotional and cognitive processing of trauma memories, hopefully reducing their intrusiveness and painful qualities and diminishing their ability to motivate problematic avoidance responses. Relational psychotherapy stresses the importance of the therapeutic relationship, especially attunement, trust, and non-judgmental methodology to address traumatic episodes. All three of these formats overlap, enabling a therapist to move between them, utilizing strengths from each to support the client. About this is the mindful awareness of the therapeutic relationship, where the therapist is aware of the subjective nature of his or her feelings, thoughts, memories, and reactions.

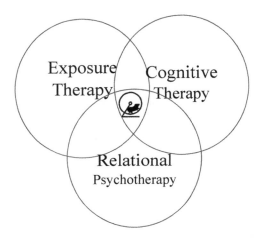

Figure 2 Psychological Methodologies to support Compassion Fatigue

In an article focusing on nursing students, by Mason and Nel (2012), compassion satisfaction had been identified and described and is coincidentally relevant to the profession of teaching and education. The authors used the Professional Quality of Life Scale-Revised IV (PQLS-RIV) to determine their findings. Professional quality of life is the ability to identify occupational hazards such as CF and burnout symptoms before they cause irreversible damage to the professional. CF is defined in the article as a state of tension or preoccupation resulting in intrusive thoughts, feelings and images—a psychological state of hyper-arousal. In other words, CF emerges as a reaction to content that professionals encounter due to the compassionate and empathetic nature of their work. CF has a sudden onset, as opposed to burnout, which has a slower onset and is regarded as a stress-related reaction to environmental demands not necessarily due to interpersonal, traumatic-laden, or compassionate contact with others. The concept of compassion satisfaction refers to the positive and potentially growth-enhancing consequences of interacting with those in situations requiring compassion and empathy. Compassion satisfaction is seen as the antithesis of CF. It is a protective factor against CF and burnout, and in spite of the pressure of CF, an individual can still have or experience high levels of compassion satisfaction. Conversely, according to Mason and Nel, the existence of symptoms of CF may serve as an impetus for professionals to seek out pleasurable and meaningful experiences in an attempt to balance out the negative consequences of distressing work. CF and burnout symptoms are not always visible in an individual, and in addition, symptoms of CF and burnout can easily be spread from an individual to other staff, resulting in a lowering of staff morale, higher turnover of staff, a dwindling of care for the profession or career, and critical lapses in professional judgment.

From a therapeutic viewpoint, who is at risk for CF? Lee et al. (2015) try to answer this very question. These authors use the Professional Quality of Life scale as well as the State-Trait Anxiety Inventory in an attempt to investigate counselor demographics and anxiety, compassion satisfaction, and burnout. Lee et al. use Figley's 1995 and 2002 (revised) model of CF, which highlights empathy erosion that comes about from repeated empathic engagement with stressful situations. Here, the professional expends effort to understand a client's experience, virtually taking on some of the client's suffering, resulting in transference for the professional and leading to an accumulation of anxiety and distress over the other's situation. This accumulation and reduced ability or interest to engage empathetically manifests in physical and psychological symptoms such as lack of energy or enthusiasm, exhaustion, a feeling of being overwhelmed, irritability, sadness, and finally, detachment from family and professional colleagues.

Therapists must be aware of the "double-edged sword" of their profession. Russell and Brickell (2015, p. 1087), and Lee et al. (2015) describe how CF can be intrusive to a therapist. Lee et al. studied 402 non-specific gender, practicing counselors. Counselor empathy is a key component to the counselor-client relationship. Lee et al. identified triggers such as delivering bad news and an inability to prevent patient suffering and speculated that certain personality traits such as wanting to be in control, wanting to be acknowledged and wanting to be a perfectionist may predispose counselors to CF. They go onto describe that counselors are at high risk for CF and are more likely to experience burnout and be self-critical, face a greater variety of difficult clinical situations, and have difficulty managing stressful events. As well, counselors can experience negative self-evaluation, demanding workloads, and difficulty coping effectively. The authors also look at select personality traits, such as dispositional optimism and locus of control. Dispositional optimism is defined as the general tendency to expect that good things rather than bad things will happen. Locus of control is defined as the degree to which individuals believe outcomes result from factors such as one's ability and effort or factors such as chance. Those counselors with low dispositional optimum and an external locus of control were at a high risk for CF. Those counselors with desire for control and perfection may be at particular risk. As well, those with an external locus of control, poor coping skills and low dispositional optimum, are at a higher risk for CF than counselors who possess an internal locus of control, effective coping skills, and a high dispositional optimum. Finally, the authors identify both types of anxiety; state and trait, related to CF. Some counselors and educators became hyper-vigilant and overly cautious to maintain control of situations and to protect themselves from uncontrolled situations to avoid dissatisfaction about themselves as professionals. Those with high trait anxiety levels may experience a stronger sense of dissatisfaction, incompetency, and loss of control.

CSI or OSI has now become the term of choice for individuals who previously have been diagnosed with labels such as professional burnout, secondary traumatic stress, vicarious traumatization, CF, and empathic distress fatigue (Russell & Brickell, 2015).

Russell and Brickell (2015) have attempted to unify the condition under one umbrella to enable clarity to occur in the diagnosis based on symptomology. They articulate that the terminology for CSI, is evidenced in biblical references, and they trace it forward through history, through WWI, WW-II, the Vietnam War, and into modern times of PTSD. They have used causal links between traumatic historical events, inferring that it has been a part of the human psyche and evolution. They give evidence the CSI can be transmitted inter-generationally as well as inter-culturally and socially (Russell & Brickell, 2015). They highlight the fact that in any encounter between two humans, transference and counter-transference are going to occur; both positive and negative. They do make the differentiation that counter-transference is often experienced in short-term within a clinical session over concerns triggered by a client's material being discussed, whereas transference occurs over a longer timeframe via repeated sharing of traumatic experiences. It is also noted that those symptoms persist outside of sessions and directly involve the mimicry of another's symptoms.

In Appendix A of their article, Russell and Brickell (2015) list multiple, overlapping signs, symptoms, and behavioral indicators for CSI. One of the reasons for this exhaustive list is that when one's empathy becomes eroded, The residual psyche can be risky and even injurious. They analyze four models to understand the workings of CSI better. These models are Figley's (1995) ten-factor causal model; McCann and Pearlman's (1999) cognitive schema model; Eriksson and Wallin's (2004) neurobiological model of burnout; and finally, Klimecki and Singer's (2012) empathic distress model. Their analysis has led them to a neu-robehavioral model of CSI. They theorize that CSI is a result of six converging lines of research. First is the development of research on imitation, mirror neurons, and emotional contagion. Second is the social psychological research of mimicry. Third is the neurobiological research of pain perception and empathy supported by Baron-Cohen (2011). Fourth is the neurobiology of the human stress response, also supported by Baron-Cohen. And, fifth is military research, which involves ancestral sequence reconstruction using DNA analysis, and combat and operational stress reaction and research into CSI itself.

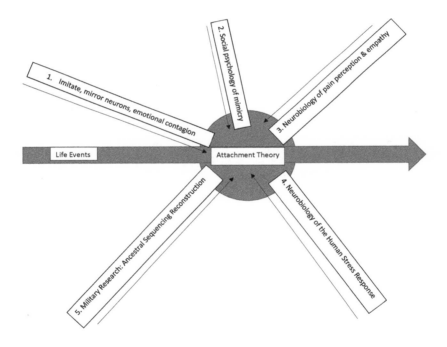

Figure 3 Neurobehavioral Model of CSI

A common thread that appears in the literature is that of Bowlby's attachment theory (1988) and Bandura's social-cognition theory (2001). Attachment theory (Bowlby, 1988) suggests that secure attachment occurs through an individual's life span, but is formulated during the development years between a child and its primary caregiver(s), both maternal and paternal. Of the three types of attachment, secure attachment is based on the knowledge that security is available and risk taking is encouraged. Avoidant attachment and anxious attachment occur when the relationship is based on negative actions or schema by the caregiver, resulting in an individual attempting to create a secure attachment in any form of relationship, usually temporary (Briere, 2012). Russell and Brickell (2015) report strong evidence which shows that infants are capable of early self and others distinction regarding emotional resonance, which is an important indicator or precursor of empathy. A positive child-caregiver relationship creates empathy, whereas a negative child-caregiver relationship does not create empathy but results in a more flattened affect and less stimulated response.

Oberle and Schonert-Reichl (2016) identify in the upper elementary/junior high setting, a developmental period where students are transitioning from family attachment towards other attachment figures such as the school and teachers who play an increasingly more important role in the early adolescent's life. Bowlby's attachment theory (1988) and Bandura's theory (1997) overlap in the educational setting, as both the teacher and child have varying degrees of attachment after their upbringing and entwined relationships. Bandura's social cognitive theory (1997) is based on self-efficacy, which is a person's belief that the person can do something and how well he or she can do it. In this theory, if a person has low-self-efficacy, that person will tend to magnify possible problems and threats and dwell on their shortcomings (Oberle & Schonert-Reichl, 2016). In Skaalvik and Skaalvik's (2016) study, they expected teacher self-efficacy to be negatively associated with teacher stress; it was, however, the opposite. They found that other significant indicators, such as prevailing goals and values of the school, which were not in alignment with the teacher's values, and a lack of supervision support negatively impacted teacher efficacy. As well, low student motivation, discipline problems, student diversity, and conflict with colleagues were also associated with low teacher efficacy. These findings are also supported by Schwarzer and Hallum (2008), showing that teacher engagement is positively associated with personal coping resources and teacher burnout is indicated by some personality characteristics including low levels of self-efficacy. In Bandura's theory, self-efficacy determines how people think, feel and act. Low self-efficacy is associated with low self-esteem and pessimistic thoughts about the self and others, as well as constructing barriers towards personal development. Positive or strong self-efficacy is associated with a strong sense of competence and cognitive processing in a variety of settings, including quality decision-making and academic achievement. People with strong self-efficacy accept and take on more challenging tasks, develop goals, and then drive to stay the course; their action plans are well thought-out and contingency plans are factored in. If a setback occurs, these individuals recover more quickly, re-establishing themselves, and create new goals or modify old ones.

Finally, Schwarzer and Hallum (2008) overlap the two theories and postulate the distinction between self-efficacy, compassion and empathy, with CSI. They suggest three aspects. First, self-efficacy implies an internal locus of control. In other words, "I am the master of my destiny." Secondly, it is future-oriented based on secure attachment, confidence of the self, and the ability to take risks. Finally, there is an operative construct at work between cognition and behaviour. Actions are thought out or reasoned through before they are implemented to move the self and subsequent organizational system forward.

CHAPTER 3
The Effects of Erosion on Cups of Empathy

Change and stress are a part of everyone's lives. Some changes are external; others are internal. Some are controllable while others are not. Some are expected while others are not. Regardless of the circumstances associated with change, stress is a by-product. The stress can be self-induced or thrust upon the individual and it may be positive or negative. What individuals or groups, small business or large corporations, and private or public institutions need to acknowledge as part of their overall structure is that change is inevitable. Stress does occur and remedial procedures and policies need to be put into place and adhered to.

The implications of Compassion Fatigue (CF) on educators are from a tri-fold perspective, sub-grouped into distinct categories. The first perspective is that of teachers and it is sub-grouped into novice educators, practicing educators or sophomores, and then experienced or senior educators.

Teacher Category: Novice

Novice teachers are those teachers immediately out of a formal training program with zero to five years of classroom experience, not including practice teaching rounds. These teachers are usually viewed as flexible, adaptable, and pliable, with a full cup of empathy and compassion. They have had little of the experience of being responsible for the successful function of a group of students or their parents, of implementing government-mandated curriculum, or of managing division-mandated paperwork. These teachers are vulnerable to CF as well as insecurity in their career choice (Merriman, 2015). They might seek external dependency and apply unrealistic expectations upon themselves. Novice professionals might doubt their training and skills; they might struggle with appropriate boundaries and make professional mistakes that could hinder their self-confidence and risk their profession (Skaalvik & Skaalvik, 2016) unless supported by supervisors or peers.

Teacher Category: Sophomore

Sophomore or practicing teachers are those who have surpassed the five-year novice mark. The five-year mark is an identifiable marker in the literature, which indicates whether educators will remain in the field. Sophomore teachers have been able to maintain employment with either an initial board or sequential boards. These teachers gain valuable "in-front-of-students" experience, deliver mandated curriculum to the best of their ability, and complete necessary paperwork required by their board and representing union. These teachers have learned to work within the system and to begin scanning horizons for different, more challenging opportunities, such as administrative or specialist settings, which require further educational training and experience.

A potential explanation for this scanning is that the level of empathy and compassion in their cups may have been lowered, and to renew their mission and purpose in life, they look for stimulating challenges to refill their cups.

These teachers, although not categorically identified by their number of years in the profession, can be grouped in the six to twenty years of experience range.

Teacher Category: Senior or Experienced

The third sub-group is that of an experienced or senior teacher. This person would have approximately twenty-one-plus years of experience. These teachers have been able to remain in the educational field regardless of internal or external pressures that may have been applied to them. On the positive side, these experienced teachers are knowledgeable in the curriculum outcomes and assessment strategies and can deal with most situations that might develop from a student, parent, or administrator standpoint. On the negative side, these seasoned teachers can also become difficult. They can become rooted in the "good old days" and refuse to modify, change, or investigate different pedagogies. They may become rigid and less pliable, and compassion and empathy reservoirs might be drained. These circumstances potentially make them a burden to the system rather than an asset. Even if they do change to keep up with the times, old habits are difficult to break, and their compassion and empathy are impacted.

The study of stress has been illustrated and termed the Yerkes-Dobson law (Figure 4) as illustrated in Posen (2013), which states that stress must increase to a certain point if one is to achieve maximum potential.

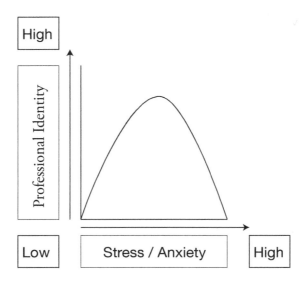

Figure 4. Yerkes-Dobson law: Stress-performance curve:
(Posen, 2013, p. 25).

This law, although using a performance indicator along the y-axis, and stress/anxiety along the x-axis, can be applied onto the experience of teaching years as illustrated in Figure 5. A novice teacher low on performance and matching years has an upward trajectory regarding performance with efficiency and efficacy, but a zone of optimal performance begins to occur in the mid-range of years teaching. After the mid-range, the performance and the efficiency begin to return to the low end. This results in extra effort and stress being required to fulfill the same job requirement the novice educator achieved.

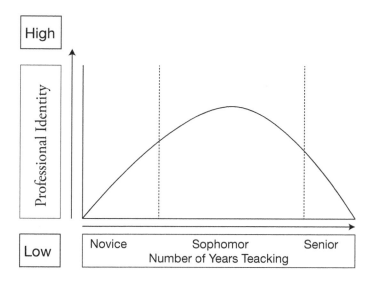

Figure 5. Teacher years of experience to performance

Administration: On site

The second perspective of CF is that of the administrator. Administrator is sub-divided into on-site administration, head-office administration, and ministry of education personnel.

Administrators on-site need to be able to discern the level of stress on-site. At a site level, one of the main responsibilities of the administrator is the health of his or her staff, both physically and psychologically. The on-site administrator must be aware of what symptoms to look for. Posen (2013) lists these symptoms as physical, intellectual, emotional, and behavioral. Physical symptoms range from mild to severe and can occur as muscular ailments, circulatory issues, digestive distress, central nervous system conditions, lymphatic lapses, fatigue, and exhaustion as well as low libido. Although the last physical symptom would be inappropriate to discuss in a supervisor-supervisee relationship, the others could be identified through record keeping regarding absenteeism of the employee. The intellectual symptoms would be evident to a supervisor as those times when an individual has trouble making decisions, has lost a sense of humor, or mentions situations of forgetfulness and difficulty concentrating on tasks. Emotional symptoms are displayed by an employee appearing nervous, anxious, tense, irritable, impatient, short-tempered, frustrated, angry, sad, apathetic, pessimistic, or cynical. For behavioral symptoms, supervisors should look for indicators of stress such as pacing, bouncing a knee while seated, fiddling with jewelry, doodling, nail-biting, compulsive eating, yelling outbursts, or blaming strategies. As Posen (2013) states, "Awareness and recognition are the first step in dealing with stress" (p. 16).

Administrators at a higher level in the supervising matrix are not adept at recognizing and dealing with stress in themselves or their employees. These individuals do, however, wield certain powers granted by their position to allow changes to occur below them in the organization, thereby allowing some stress relief. What these individuals need to be aware of is that they can control the amount of work-related pressure that could result in an individual reaching his or her "tipping point." Posen (2013) defines the tipping point as when the pressure exceeds individuals' level of tolerance and they become exhausted, collapse, or snap. At this point, the vessel of empathy and compassion is capsized and submerged.

Administration: Head-Office

The implication for administrators at head-office level is to understand stress and how it is cyclical. There is research in Posen

(2013) describing a healthy stress cycle, which involves periods of stress interspersed with periods of rest, relaxation, and recovery. During downtime, the body can restore energy and recovery from exertions caused by the stress. This description can be overlaid upon various time frames ranging from grandiose to minuscule. The perpetual stress response or the chronic stress syndrome (Posen, 2013) is the same description as the Health Stress Cycle, however, instead of time for recovery and recuperation, this time is occupied with more stress-producing initiative, as well as planning and preparing for the next round of stress. As a result, the peaks of stress increase sequentially, and the erosion of empathy and compassion run counter to this trend.

Head-office administrators need to enlighten themselves regarding stress and its implications. They must set aside sufficient time to allow for recovery and recuperation to occur. They must set schedules that are flexible to allow for downtime and decompression on a daily, weekly, monthly, and yearly basis.

Administration: Government Bureaucracy

The final level of administration is that of the Ministry of Education. This bureaucratic level is responsible for curriculum development and design, certification of teachers, and education programs, as well as monitoring trends in the professional sphere of education. In Posen (2013), he emphasizes that many bureaucrats or senior management officials believe that the concept of increased velocity of change is best for a system, when in reality an increase of implementation speed does not release the pressure of stress but compounds it. The ministry level is accountable to the electorate, which can be a major cause of pressure and stress upon the system. An administrator is a person who is responsible for the smooth operation of an institution, whether it be public, private, business, or service industry. The role of the administrator in an organization is, in my opinion, supported by Merriman (2015), to prevent the flow of pressure coming down the proverbial pipe and to act as a check valve for parental, patient, or customer dissatisfaction from moving upward through the pipe. Also, they are to act as release valves at each level of the organization, allowing pent-up pressure to be discharged, thereby reducing the levels of stress. Merriman lists supervisor strategies as multi-fold. They include modeling internal focus; developing and monitoring staffs' self-care plans; discussing self-validation with staff; having an open discussion of self-doubts; having a discussion regarding boundaries, professional and personal; encouraging self-exploration and reinforcing self-awareness; assisting in normalizing the experience of CF symptoms; discussing these same symptoms and risks; reviewing self-care standards that might be in policy and procedures; addressing adverse experiences; educating staff about protective factors; encouraging staff to keep a journal on compassion satisfaction; and, providing a supportive, safe, caring, and encouraging environment. Merriman also lists protective factors that administrators and supervisors can enlist to support staff. These are to identify compassion-satisfaction situations; to educate members regarding CF as well as educate higher administrators about the need for supervision; to allow for consulting and debriefing to occur on a regular basis, either officially or unofficially; and to allow for peer support to occur and to make staff aware of appropriate boundaries. Finally, Merriman suggests incorporating professional development in self-awareness, self-reflection, and self-care.

Administrators should not allow for the free flowing of materials from higher levels of administration, nor should they act as additional means of supplying pressure. They must regulate the pressure of changes mandated from top-level administrators, enabling a smooth transition to occur when new curriculum is implemented and changes are necessary. They must act as check valves, which allow material to flow through at a prescribed rate. An example of this is when government bureaucrats monitoring trends in education shift the focus of a subject's curriculum based on research that is flawed or incomplete. The example used in this document is that of the pyramid of interventions (Hoglund et al., 2015; Oakes et al., 2013), which was a theory based on action research that claimed to improve literacy rates. This strategy, however, adds more pressure, stress, and workload to educators, resulting in an expenditure of valuable tax dollars toward professional training time for educators, increasing stress towards the tipping point, and compounding the inefficiency cycle.

For material moving up the pipe of the organization, the client, which could be a student, parent, or community, the administrator must act as a pressure-release valve for the client by using problem-solving skills and communication strategies and by being knowledgeable of circumstances, situations, and curriculum. These administrators can release the built-up pressure and stress harmlessly, without significant damage occurring to the organization, its purpose, its staff, or the community.

Professional Therapists:

The third and final perspective regarding the implications section of this paper is that of the professional therapist. This perspective is subdivided into signs and symptoms of CF; support for those suffering from CF; and finally, a means of rebuilding the compassion and empathy for these individuals. Four tools of strength building are explored in the recommendation section of this paper.

Signs of empathy erosion and CF can be subtle or pronounced. As stated earlier, CF can occur from a single traumatic event, or it can occur because of small, insignificant, repetitive events that slowly erode the empathy and compassion. An individual may voluntarily or involuntarily seek help from a professional therapist. Regardless, the therapist must be able to watch for signs-physical, psychological, social, or behavioral that are indications of CF. The therapist, by using observational techniques and detailed record keeping, asking insightful and conscientious questions, listening with intention, and building significant trust and rapport with a client, can begin the task of servicing the client.

All the literature reviews basically listed the same symptoms, and though they may have different descriptions they all point towards the erosion of empathy and CF. Posen (2013) sums up signs to watch for. Physically, they are head-ache, clenching of the jaw or grinding of teeth, muscle tightness in the neck and/ or shoulders, lower back pain or stiffness, palpitations of the circulatory system, pain or pressure in the chest, nausea with or without vomiting, unexplained abdominal cramps, irregularity of the bowels, frequent washroom use, irregular menstrual cycles for women, sweating of the palms or soles, a feeling of unsteadiness or shakiness, chronic fatigue and exhaustion, a loss or increase of appetite, difficulty sleeping, and a loss of interest in sex.

Intellectual or psychological symptoms are listed by Posen (2013) as trouble concentrating; forgetfulness; difficulty in making large or small decisions; loss of humor; complaints of racing thoughts or the opposite—a blank, empty feeling.

Posen (2013) then highlights emotional and social symptoms as a feeling of anxiousness; being tense, irritable, and impatient; being short-tempered, easily frustrated, or quick to display anger; a feeling of sadness or depression; a loss of interest in things that once excited them; a change from optimism to constant pessimism and cynicism regarding all aspects of their life; and low self-esteem. Finally, Posen outlines behavioral symptoms such as fidgeting, knee bouncing, pacing, a feeling of agitation or restlessness, trouble sitting still and relaxing, and more pronounced nervous habits such as nail-biting, playing with jewelry, or excessive doodling, compulsive eating or smoking, drinking, uncharacteristic yelling and swearing, and blaming others for their problems.

In the effort to support a client, the therapist must understand the history of the client's situation. The family, medical and work history will allow the therapist to get a better overview of what may be factors leading to stress. The specific medical history can be retrieved with permission if the therapist is working in an accredited health facility, or if a general history can be generated from the client. A genogram of the family history can be created to determine potential genetic factors of causation. Also, a work history can be obtained so that specific sources of stress at or from work can be identified. These factors, according to Cooper and Kahn (2013), could be intrinsic to the job, such as poor physical work conditions, work overload, time pressure, or physical danger. Sources of stress at work could also include the role of the individual in the organization. Is there role ambiguity, role conflict, or a responsibility for people? Career development can also be a factor, where one is over-promoted, under-promoted, feeling a lack of job security, or feeling that ambitions have been restricted or held-back. Another source causing stress at work might be relationships. Does the individual have poor work relations? These could be with supervisor, colleagues, or subordinates to the client. About organizational structure—is it causing stress? Is little or no participation allowed in important decision-making? Are office politics occurring or is a specific restriction being placed on behavior of staff? Finally, does the individual have a work-life balance, where family problems and life crises are allowed time to be dealt with, or does the client have to put work responsibilities first and foremost above all other responsibilities?

These six critical areas of questioning are used to support the client in times of stress. By asking questions in the six areas, the therapist can support and begin to assist the client in developing strategies to cope with stressors at work and begin planning achievable goals that can be designed to give hope to the client from a trusted advocate.

As the planning stages of therapy begin to emerge, the focus for the therapist will be to highlight and assist the client in identifying strengths. To do so, four valid and reliable psychometric tools are suggested. The first, specifically for educators, is the Teacher Stress Inventory (TSI) (Fimian, 1998).

Second is a tool to measure occupational stress and the pressure it evokes called the Pressure Management Indicator (Williams & Cooper, 1998), which evolved from the Occupational Stress Indicator. These tools would confirm the evidence of stress in the individual's life and assist in constructing therapeutic goals.

The third tool is the Myers-Briggs Personality Inventory (MBPI) (Tuel & Betz, 1998). This tool would be utilized to assist the client in re-establishing a personal belief and values system, enabling the client to begin refilling his/her cup of compassion and re-establishing empathy. The fourth and final tool is the Strong Interest Inventory Profile (SIIP) (Strong, Donnay, Morris, Schaubhut & Thompson, 2008), which would be utilized to guide and assist clients to achieve goals through an awareness of hope.

CHAPTER 4
My Personal Cup of Empathy

I have been an elementary generalist educator with the same school division throughout my thirty-year career. I have had the opportunity to educate children in a culturally homogeneous society, as well as in mainstream public educational settings. I am a heterosexual male educator who is approaching retirement. My self-positioning for this paper is to acknowledge that change does occur, personally and professionally; sometimes it is within our control of influence, sometimes, it is beyond. My position about CSI and burnout is that I have experienced both. My experience started from a significant traumatic event at work that overtook my teaching career, family life, and future career aspirations.

As others also acknowledge, I knew that teaching was a stressful career choice (Hakanen, Bakker, & Schaufeli, 2006; Russell, Altmaier, & Velzen, 1987), however, at the onset of my teaching career, I had a full cup of empathy, a passion to teach youth, support from administration, and collegial support. I was eager, enthusiastic, and efficient. In the beginning, I was the "master of my destiny." I was in staff positions that allowed for autonomous decision making, provided it was in the best interest of the students, affordable, and could be seamlessly incorporated into the everyday legislated curriculum requirements.

I was fortunate to make it past the early years of teaching, which research suggests are the primary years where teachers resign from their position for a multitude of reasons (Hoglund et al., 2015; Oakes et al., 2013; Randler et al., 2014; Russell et al., 1987; Schwarzer & Hallum, 2008; Skaalvik & Skaalvik, 2016). These include reasons such as disciplinary problems, student apathy, over-crowded classrooms, involuntary transfers, excessive paperwork, inadequate salaries, demanding or unsupportive parents, and lack of administrative support (Russell et al., 1987). These, plus the job-demands model (Hakanen et al., 2006) of incorporating more legislative requirements, caused me to work harder and to put in longer hours to maintain my self-efficacy as a competent, caring, and compassionate educator. This need to work harder and longer, detached and isolated, in an almost all-female staff, was the beginning of the erosion of my cup of empathy (Lee, McCarthy, Veach, MacFarlane & Leroy, 2014).

CF, another term for CSI, is the silent eroding of one's values and beliefs, which slowly undermines an individual's efficacy, both internally and externally. Hoglund et al., (2015) support this by identifying three dimensions that can affect an individual: *job-related emotional exhaustion, depersonalization*, and a *lack of a sense of personal accomplishment*. These three dimensions can negatively impact classroom instruction quality and discipline techniques.

A series of events occurred during my teaching career that contributed to burnout. First was job-related emotional stress and exhaustion as a result of directives from central office administrators that were contrary to my own educational beliefs and values. I strove to incorporate these directives to the best of my professional capabilities, and fortunately, the on-site administrator had the same value and belief system and was not afraid to challenge the directive from central office.

Depersonalization, which is the second marker defined by Lee et al. (2015), is a loss of locus of control and dispositional optimum. Dispositional optimum is the general tendency to expect that good rather than bad things will happen, and locus of control is the degree to which one's belief outcomes result from factors inside and outside one's ability and effort. "Low dispositional optimum and an external locus of control…result in a higher risk of compassion fatigue" (p. 360). I expected that good things would come my way, such as career advancement, because I value strong work ethic, kept abreast of new ideas and educational philosophy, and was passionate about teaching and caring for children. External forces, however, were not synchronized to my values or beliefs. Slowly, my internal optimism of my capabilities, values and beliefs began to erode. I attempted to increase my professional experience and external locus of control by applying for administrative positions in and out of the division but found myself always coming up short. Then came the traumatic event.

Symptoms of anxiety began to manifest as I disengaged from job and work-related projects. I experienced a lowering of energy and enthusiasm and more exhaustion, feeling overwhelmed, irritable, and detached from my family (Lee et al., 2015). On top of this, a principal, whom I admired and respected, retired. He was replaced by an individual who made critical changes to the functioning of a well-respected community school, which affected its culture and environment. The changes he began to incorporate were supported by central office, and he soon became a favorite of top administrators.

The third marker, loss of a sense of personal accomplishment, began with this new principal, who undermined me when in a private meeting he challenged my teaching ability based on provincial test results as well as his in-class observations. He removed me from my classroom duties and created another position within the school setting that he said would be more suited to my abilities. I eventually found myself suffering from state and trait anxiety. State anxiety is the subjective feeling of tension, apprehension, nervousness, and worry. Trait anxiety is based on the intensity and frequency of an individual's experience and proneness to anxiety (Lee et al., 2015). In their mediation analysis article, Schwarzer and Hallum (2008) found that teacher self-efficacy was a personal resource factor to protect against the experience of job stress and thus makes burnout less likely. This new teaching role, however, quickly undermined my teacher self-efficacy resource, and because there was lack of administrative and peer support since I was working in isolation from the rest of the staff, further erosion of my self-efficacy occurred. Discipline and control of student behavior in the school as a whole became lax as the school philosophy changed from one of respect of the child to one of sympathy with the child.

Before the new administrator had arrived, the philosophy of the school was child-centered, and a collaborative approach was taken by all staff to develop programs for students below grade level. This programming involved a resource room staffed with a qualified resource teacher, who conducted small-group work in a pull-out program developing students' necessary skills for success. The new administrator removed the small pull-out resource room and the qualified teacher and implemented a tiered pyramid of support (Oakes et al., 2013). The pyramid of support involved weekly or monthly meetings to discuss student progress. This change resulted in students remaining below grade level, as they stayed in the classroom with only teacher support, or sometimes with an educational assistant depending upon the severity of the student's need and the school's budget. As the school was now deemed a professional learning community, teachers were required to attend professional development meetings to implement the new philosophy. This resulted in a revolving door of substitute teachers, more after-hours' preparation time, and more documentation for a new student reading program. In my professional opinion, the discipline and control of the school had never been an issue. But now, with the changes in philosophy, constant interruptions for meetings, and the presence of substitute teachers moving throughout the building, staff and students were constantly in a state of flux. The philosophy of the school changed from a caring, nurturing environment to one of data-driven, top-down, bureaucratic chaos.

This change in school philosophy led to a traumatic event in my professional career. While verbally disciplining a student known for bullying his peers, whom I had myself witnessed physically assaulting another student, I touched him by reaching out and giving him a single finger tap to the forehead, for lying directly to me. This seemingly small event of discipline escalated into a full-fledged investigation by authority figures and was spearheaded by the new administrator. As a result, I experienced an emotional and physical breakdown, which took months of recuperation and negotiations, before a mutually satisfactory ending for all parties involved. I liken it to a ship being capsized in a heavy storm with high seas. My career was capsized, and once righted, it required many months of psychological therapy and physical healing as well as antidepressants and strong family and peer support to eventually restart my journey toward being an educator whose values, beliefs, and self-efficacy were once again intact.

At one point, I seriously considered leaving the profession of education (Skaalvik & Skaalvik, 2016), but I persevered for three reasons. First, finding another career path would take due diligence and time to become a qualified professional, which would require financial planning, psychological energy, and family support. Second, I am a compassionate individual whose life work has been working with children, and I did not want to give that up. And, third, leaving the field of education or that school division was not a viable option at the time due to financial and family responsibilities. Plus, the administrator who undermined me would have been successful in accomplishing his goal of removing me from my passion for teaching and education.

As to the self-positioning section of this paper, I know of what I speak and research. I am happy to say that my ship was righted and all the water was successfully bailed out. I have been able to re-start my educational journey on my terms and re-establish my self-efficacy. I am well aware that once the ship has been capsized, it can happen again. However, with the help of psycho-educational assistance, I am better able to recognize the signs of when CSI and burnout are beginning to affect my cup of empathy.

Today, my compassion satisfaction is at a high level for two reasons. First, I am six months away from retiring from teaching. Secondly, I have been challenging myself by working towards another degree in psychological counseling so that I can commence another profession after teaching.

CHAPTER 5
Refilling the Cup of Empathy

The recommendations for therapists and those in supervisory positions of educators are three-fold; first is to be able to recognize the symptoms of CF in their clients and employees and to appreciate and understand that the injury can occur after a single traumatic event or over a longer timeframe of small and seemingly less significant events. Therapists and supervisors will recognize the symptoms as a reduced capacity for or interest in the individual's duties or responsibilities. There can also be the perception of a loss of locus of control within the individual's immediate environment, which is the loss of autonomy within professional and personal spheres. Finally, the disposition optimum may be affected, resulting in the tendency to expect that bad things rather than good will occur.

The second recommendation is for therapists and supervisors to provide the necessary supports to assist those individuals who have indicators of CF. These supports from a therapist's perspective would be in the form of documentary evidence such as the Teacher Stress Inventory (TSI), the Occupational Stress Inventory (OSI), and the Myers-Briggs Personality Inventory (MBI). These tools would be used to determine a level of stress that the individual might be encountering. The TSI has a reliability factor of .93 and is considered valid for determining stress amongst educators (Fimian, 1998; Fimian & Fastenau, 1990). The OSI, which is for general occupations, has a reliability factor of .80 and is considered to have strong internal and external validity (Evers, Frese & Cooper, 2000; Kahn & Cooper, 1991). Two other tools that can also be used during therapy by a trained therapist are the Strong Interest Index Profile (SIIP) and the MBPI. The SIIP has a reliability factor of .87 and is a valid tool for enlightening and reaffirming an individual's strengths and interests, potentially opening new avenues of career options or reaffirmation of the chosen career (Strong et al., 2008). The MBPI tool is considered valid and reliable with a factor of .84 to .88, and it enables dialogue to occur between the therapist and client about personality traits and life and career expectations (Tuel & Betz, 1998). Both of these tools would be used in conjunction with each other to re-establish the individual's values and beliefs as well in their purpose.

The third recommendation for therapists is to advocate on behalf of clients to service providers of extended health-care benefits. This ensures that coverage is continued and maintained until clients can return to their chosen occupations or are able to move forward on new career paths with their cups of empathy refilled.

From a supervisory standpoint of educators, the supervisor must acknowledge that teaching at all levels is a stressful occupation (Hakanen et al., 2006; Randler et al., 2015; Russell et al., 1987). The supervisor must remain neutral in a situation of CF illness. Both site and head-office administrators must appreciate five significant indicators when supervising individuals. First, be aware of the difference between good stress, also called eustress, which is productive, and distress, which leads to exhaustion, illness, and breakdown. In doing so, corporations, administrators, employees, and individuals must determine the comfort zone for optimal production before the hump is reached (Posen, 2013).

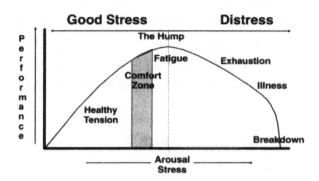

Figure 6. The human function curve:
The hump. (Posen, 2013, p. 90).

The hump is the peak of healthy tension leading into the comfort zone where optimal performance and production occur. Once the optimal performance is achieved or produced, a downward trend develops until a period of recovery can occur. Posen (2013) refers to this as the human function curve. At the hump, three things occur: first is the loss of energy; second is a decrease in performance; and third is a loss of insight.

The second significant indicator is about the hump, itself. How many times is it occurring in the corporation? And, how often are administrators and staff asked to perform past the hump? Third, if the hump has been breached, as in certain situations it must be, then sufficient time for recovery must be allowed. The fourth factor when the hump is breached is based on time: the longer an individual or group is metaphorically out past the hump, the longer the recovery time. The fifth significant factor involves a change in personal and corporate philosophy. The old philosophy when the hump is crossed was to push through to the end until completed, working longer and harder to achieve something. Working past the hump is counterproductive. Posen (2013) refers to this as the inefficiency cycle, where one is fatigued upon crossing the hump, is inefficiently productive, puts in longer hours, and gets less sleep and leisure time, thereby reinforcing the fatigue.

CHAPTER 6
Safeguarding Cups of Empathy

The fundamental next steps that I envision for Compassion Fatigue (CF) and empathy erosion as they apply to the field of education, are three-fold. First, look at how the role of Bowlby's attachment therapy impacts the student-teacher relationships (Briere, 2002; Briere, 2012; Hoglund et al., 2015; Lee et al., 2015; Oberle & Schonert-Reichl, 2016; Randler et al., 2015; Russell & Brickell, 2015; Schwarzer & Hallum, 2008; Skaalvik & Skaalvik, 2016). Both individuals carry their unique form of attachment, and a study could be conducted to evaluate how attachment could act as a defensive mechanism against empathy erosion or could be a potential indicator of future CF. I envision this study to be in the form of a confidential survey for educators that would ask specific questions related to their personal feeling of attachment (Kyriacou, 2001; Russell et al., 1987). It would also ask questions about their relationships with others in the work environment, such as the children they teach, their peers, supervisors, and immediate family. At this point, I envision this survey as a combination of the questions above. Results would be placed on a seven-point Likert scale and then subsequently statistically analyzed. Ultimately, this would be a computer-based survey that would generate immediate results for the individual. The purpose of this study would allow for potential screening of educators who might be approaching the hump and might, therefore, be prone to CF and emotional erosion, thereby allowing for preventive and proactive steps to occur.

The second fundamental next step is to study if there is statistical evidence of a linear or causal relationship between CF or empathy erosion and teacher stress. The hypothesis is that as the stress increases, empathy and compassion decrease proportionally. I envision on the x-axis, the measurement of stress on a scale of zero through ten, with zero indicating no stress and ten indicating severe stress. On the y-axis is a measurement of compassion and empathy, with a scale of zero to ten; here, the ten at the top of the axis would indicate a complete vessel filled with empathy and erosion, while the zero end would indicate no compassion or empathy left in the vessel. This second study would enlist the use of statistically valid and reliable tools to measure CF such as the Professional Quality of Life-Compassion Satisfaction, Revision III (Sprang et al., 2007; Zeidner et al., 2013). The stress tool to specifically measure teacher stress would be the TSI. The TSI would also be supported by the Pressure Management Inventory (PMI), which would allow for a measurement of individual in supervisory positions. Finally, the OSI would also be incorporated to further support the hypothesis.

The third portion of what I envision to be next is to disseminate the information to a wide audience but specifically focusing on the field of education. The literature shows that there have been many attempts to study the phenomenon of CF in the health industry and with these attempts, documents and tools have been developed. However, in education, the tools developed are not used on a regular basis, and it would be valuable if they were. For example, the TSI should be used on a regular basis for monitoring stress levels in educators, supervisors, and the organization as a whole. This would allow for preemptive and proactive planning to support and assist individuals on the brink of the tipping point.

CHAPTER 7
My Phoenix Rising: A Returning of Self-Worth & Refilling a Cup of Empathy

I can say that I have been down the path of occupational and compassionate stress injury. I have experienced the slow erosion of my cup of empathy. This erosion eventually reached a point where it devoured my core belief and values system and impacted both my professional and personal integrity. But there is and has been a degree of hope throughout the journey.

With the assistance of doctors, therapists, union and legal representatives, and a strong spouse and family, plus the intellectual challenge of a counseling program, I have been able to right my ship and begin moving forward again.

The literature highlights mindfulness as a requirement for combating the phenomenon of CF and occupational stress. I would postulate, however, that this is just one piece of the puzzle. Mindfulness is sufficient if one can recognize the stressors in life and can take steps to ward off the trait and state levels of anxiety. However, when the intensity of the fatigue syndrome occurs either through rapid onset or time lapse occurrence, mindfulness is not enough (Kelloway, 2017). The other pieces of the puzzle to combat the syndrome are medical interventions through prescriptions, if necessary; therapists trained in a variety of counseling strategies; other professionals specializing in legal and/or ethical matters; supportive and understanding family structure with roots embedded in a strong foundation; and an intellectually challenging endeavor of interest with a purpose or goal in mind.

I have been able to right my cup of empathy, refill it with compassion, and move forward personally and professionally. I am extremely grateful to all those I have encountered who have supported me on this journey, and I am looking forward to moving ahead into the field of counseling.

CHAPTER 8
Conclusion

CF and empathy erosion are real. There are many different names for the phenomenon of burnout, such as CF, vicarious trauma, professional burnout, secondary traumatic stress, empathy distress fatigue, OSI, CSI, and empathy erosion, plus PTSD. It is a psychological disorder caused by trauma. There are also tools that have been designed to highlight, track, and focus on ways and means of controlling, monitoring, and assisting with it. But what they all have in common is the human psychic capacity of empathy. There is only a limited amount of empathy or compassion that one can utilize, and without sufficient time to regenerate the spent psychic energy, severe health issues can occur. Tools have been categorically assigned to measure this phenomenon, but the key that is missing is how professionals in their chosen fields allow themselves to get to the tipping point. Regardless of the tool, once CF is identified, steps must be outlined and adhered to, so sufficient repair and refilling of the cup of empathy can occur.

The condition of Compassion Fatigue is not without its naysayers, who suggest that individuals, corporations, and institutions must work through it. The phenomenon is camouflaged by statements such as "suck it up," "get over it," "work through it," or even, "just do it." In the short term this may work, but at what cost?

I fear that the all-important financial bottom-line shall continue to be a sole motivation for major corporations, educational ministries, institutions, and entities to continue attempting to justify more demands, more expectations, and longer hours dedicated to the job by the staff. This philosophy of big business at the cost of eroded cups of empathy, reduced compassion, fatigue, self-doubt, depression, and even suicide, must be curtailed.

Change in life is inevitable, and life is not a static event. People, for the most part, move into professional occupations, including education, wanting to make a difference. They come to their chosen fields full of their values and belief systems as well as full cups of compassion and empathy. But one constant related to the existence of change in professional and personal life-cycles is time. Time can be a catalyst allowing for change to occur, or it can be a dam blocking change from happening. In the first instance, time as a catalyst for change can either be slow or fast. If change happens too slowly, practitioners can become outdated, leaving them out-of-the-loop and feeling frustrated and anxious, questioning their professionalism. If it occurs too quickly, time can alter perception of what is best for the client. Change that occurs too rapidly leaves the affected members off-balance and struggling to understand how this change is overall beneficial to the system as a whole. An example of this is how schools have become a clearing house for publications marketing the latest trends in education. Exorbitant amounts of tax dollars are placed in operating budgets and subsequently spent on these new curriculum materials and technology to replace the existing materials, which have been declared as out-date and therefore no longer useful in delivering curriculum. Educators are then expected to immediately work these new materials into the daily routine of educating students. This mandated requirement causes stress, anxiety, and frustration, and begins the inefficiency cycle, which in turn leads towards perpetual stress response, also known as the chronic stress syndrome. Chronic stress syndrome is when the individual is constantly on duty and in a state of fight-or-flight response to threats. The threat, in this case, is the constant change in curriculum and technologies, with the expectation of professional accountability and responsibilities to students, peers, supervisors and the public.

On a positive note, there are valid and reliable tools that have been developed to identify when an individual is undergoing stress. These tools, from a general to a specific profession, are the OSI, the Pressure Management Indicator and then, for educators specifically, the TSI. Plus, there is the Yerkes-Dobson law regarding positive stress and how it can be used to maintain a health stress cycle. This occurs when an individual recognizes that time is needed to change, adapt, and work effectively to implement the changes. Also, when approaching the hump, which is the peak of optimal performance, indicators of stress must be dealt with to allow the mind and body to decompress from the stress and rejuvenate the psyche.

A Benjamin Franklin quote, "An ounce of prevention is worth a pound of cure!" basically states that if the tools above are utilized effectively, less time and money would be spent healing the sick, or refilling the cup of empathy and compassion.

REFERENCES

Adams, R. E., Figley, C. R., & Boscarino, J. A. (2008). The Compassion Fatigue Scale: Its use with social workers following urban disaster. *Research on Social Work Practice, 18(3)*, 238- 250.doi:10.1177/1049731509310190

Babble, S. (2012, January 4). Find a therapist. Retrieved October 17, 2016 from https://www.psychologytoday.com/blog/somatic-psycholgy/201207/compassion- fatigue

Bandura, A. (2001). Social cognitive theory: An agentic perspective. *Annual Review of Psychology, 52,* p. 1-26. Retrieved from https://www.uky.edu/~eushe2/Bandura/Bandura2001ARPr.pdf

Baron-Cohen, S. (2011). *The science of evil: On empathy and the origins of cruelty.* New York, NY: Basic.

Beaumont, E., Durkin, M., Hollins-Martin, C., & Carson, J. (2015). Measuring relationships between self-compassion, compassion fatigue, burnout and well-being in student counselors and student cognitive behavioral psychotherapists: A quantitative survey. *Counselling and Psychotherapy Research 16(1),* 15-23.doi:10.1002/capr.12054

Berger, K. S. (2011). *The developing person through the lifespan* (8th ed.) New York, NY: Worth.

Berzoff, J., & Kita, E. (2010). Compassion fatigue and counter-transference: Two different concepts. *Clinical Social Work Journal, 38*(3), 341-49. doi:10.1007/s10615-010-027-8

Bhutani, J., Bhutani, B., Sukriti, Y. P., & Kalra, S. (2012). Compassion fatigue and burnout amongst clinicians: A medical exploratory study. *Indian Journal of Psychological Medicine 34*(4), 332-337. doi:10.4103/0253-7176.108206

Bowlby, J. (1978). Attachment theory and its therapeutic implications. *Adolescent Psychiatry 6*, 5-33.

Bowlby, J. (1988). *A secure base: Parent-child attachment and healthy human development.* New York, NY: Basic Books.

Briere, J. (2012). Working with trauma: Mindfulness and compassion. In C. K. Germer & R. D. Siegel (Eds.), *Compassion and wisdom in psychotherapy* (pp. 265-279). New York, NY: Guilford.

Chirkowska-Smolak, T., & Kleka, P. (2011). The Maslach Burnout Inventory-General Survey: Validation across different occupational groups in Poland. *Polish Psychological Bulletin 42*(2), 86-94. doi:10.2478/v10059-011-0014-x

Cooper, C. L., & Cartwright, S. (1994). Healthy mind; healthy organization—A proactive approach to occupational stress.*HumanRelations,47*(4),455-473. http://dx.doi.org/10.1177/001872679404700405

Cooper, G. & Kahn, H. (2013). *50 things you can do today to manage stress at work.* West Sussex, United Kingdom: Summersdale.

Cormier, S., Nurius, P. S., & Osborne, C. J. (2013). *Interviewing and strategies for helpers.* (7th ed.). Belmont, CA: Brook/Cole Cengage Learning.

Craig, C. D., & Sprang G. (2010). Compassion satisfaction, compassion fatigue, and burnout in a national sample of trauma treatment therapists. *Anxiety, Stress and Coping 23*(3), 319-339. doi:10.1080/10615800903085818

Edinger, L.V., Houts, P. L., Meyer, D. V. & Sand, O. (1981). *Education in the 80's-Curricular challenges.* Washington, DC: National Education Association.

Elangovan, A. R., Auer-Rizzi, W., & Szabo, E. (2015). It's the act that counts: Minimizing post-violation erosion of trust. *Leadership and Organization Development Journal 36*(1), 81-96. doi:10.1108/LODJ-07-2012-0090

Eriksson, P. S., & Wallin, L. (2004). Functional consequences of stress-related suppression of adult hippocampal neurogenesis-A novel hypothesis on the neurobiology of burnout. *Acta Neurol Scand 110,* 275-280. doi:10.1111/j.1600-0404.2004.00328.x

Evers, A., Frese, M., & Cooper, C. L. (2000). Revisions and further developments of the Occupational Stress Indicator: LISREL results from four Dutch studies. *Journal of Occupational and Organizational Psychology, 73*(2), 221–240. doi:10.1348/096317900166994

Figley, C. R. (1995). *Compassion fatigue: Coping with secondary traumatic stress disorder in those who treat the traumatized.* New York: Brunner-Routledge.

Figley, C. R. (2002). Compassion fatigue: Psychotherapists' chronic lack of self-care. *Journal of Clinical Psychology, 58*(11), 1433-1441. doi:10.1002/jclp.10090 Fimian, M. J. (1998). *Teacher Stress Inventory.* Brandon, VT: Clinical Psychology Publishing

Fimian, M. J., & Fastenau, P. S. (1990). The validity and reliability of the Teacher Stress Inventory: A re-analysis of aggregate data. *Journal of Organizational Behaviour, 11*(2), 151-157. doi:10.1002/job.4030110206

Freudanberger, H. J. (1975). The staff burn-out syndrome in alternative institutions. *Psychotherapy: Theory, Research & Practice 12*(1), 73-82. http://dx.doi.org/10.1037/h0086411

Froese-Germain, B. (2014). Work-life balance and the Canadian teaching profession. *Canadian Teachers' Federation*, 1–10. Retrieved from http://files.eric.ed.gov/fulltext/ED546884.pdf

Gleichgerrcht, E., & Decety, J. (2013). Empathy in clinical practice: How individual dispositions, gender, and experience moderate empathic concern, burnout, and emotional distress in physicians. *PLoS One 8*(4), 1-12. doi:10.1371/journal.pone.0061526

Gold, J. (2011). Bowlby's attachment theory. In S. Goldstein & J. A. Naglieri (Eds.), *Encyclopedia of Child Behaviour and Development* (pp. 272-275). New York, NY: Springer Science & Business Media.

Hakanen, J. J., Bakker, A. B., & Schaufeli, W. B., (2006). Burnout and work engagement among teachers. *Journal of School Psychology, 43*(6), 495-513. doi:10.1016/j.jsp.2005.11.001

Hoglund, W. L. G., Klingle, K. E. & Hosan, N. E. (2015). Classroom risks and resources: Teacher burnout, classroom quality and children's adjustment in high needs elementary schools. *Journal of School Psychology, 53*(5), 337-357. http://dx.doi.org/10.1016/j.jjsp.2015.06.002

Kahn, H. & Cooper, C. L. (1991). A note on the validity of the mental health and coping scales of the Occupational Stress Indicator. *Stress Medicine, 7*(3), 185-187. doi:10.1002/smi.2460070310

Kahneman, D. (2013). *Thinking, fast and slow.* New York, NY: Farrar, Straus and Giroux. Kelloway, E. K. (2017). Mental health in the workplace: Towards evidence-based practice. *Journal of Canadian Psychology, 52*(1), 1-6.

Klimecki, O., & Singer, T. (2012). Empathic distress fatigue rather than compassion fatigue? Integrating findings from empathy research in psychology and social neuroscience. In B. Oakley, A. Knafo, G. Madhaven, & D. S. Wilson (Eds.), *Pathological altruism.* (pp. 368-383). New York, NY: Oxford University Press.

Kyriacou, C. (2001). Teacher stress: Directions for future research. *Educational Review, 53*(1), 27-35. doi:10.1080/0013191 0120033628

Lee, W., McCarthy-Veach, P., Macfarlane, I. M., & Leroy, B. S. (2015). Who is at risk for compassion fatigue? An investigation of genetic counselor demographics, anxiety, compassion satisfaction, and burnout. *Journal of Genetic Counseling, 24*(2), 358- 370. doi:10.1007/s10897-014-9716-5

Levitin, D. J. (2014). *The organized mind: Thinking straight in the age of information overload.* London, England: Penguin.

Llewellyn, H. A. (2009). *An exploratory study of the relationship between compassion fatigue and empathy in professional counselors.* (Doctoral dissertation). Retrieved from http://rave.ohiolink.edu/etdc/view?acc_num=ohiou1255965589

Maslach, C. (1976). Burned-out. *Human Behaviour, 9*(5), 16-22.

Maslach, C., Schaufeli, W. B., & Leiter, M. P. (2001). Job burnout. *Annual Review of Psychology, 52*(1), 397-422. doi:10.1146/annurev.psych.52.1.397

Mason, H. D., & Nel, J. A. (2012). Compassion fatigue, burnout, and compassion satisfaction: Prevalence among nursing students. *Journal of Psychology in Africa, 22*(3), 451-456. doi:1 0.1080/143302237.2012.10820554? journalCode=rpia20

McCann, I. L. & Pearlman, L. A. (1997). Vicarious traumatization: A framework for understanding the psychological effects of working with victims. *Journal of Traumatic Stress, 3*(1), 131-149. doi:10.1002/jts.2490030110

McGuire, W. H. (1981). Teacher stress and burnout. In L. V. Edinger, P. L. Houts, & D. V. Meyer (Eds.), *Education in the 80's.* (pp. 62–70). Washington. DC: National Education Association.

Merriman, J. (2015). Enhancing counselor supervision through compassion fatigue education. *Journal of Counseling and Development, 93*(3), 370-378. doi:10.1002/jcad.12035 Negash, S., & Sahin, S. (2011). Compassion fatigue in marriage and family therapy: Implications for therapists and clients. *Journal of Marital and Family Therapy, 37*(1), 1-13.

Oakes, W. P., Lane, K. L., Jenkins, A., & Booker, B. B. (2013). Three-tiered models of prevention: Teacher efficacy and burnout. *Education and Treatment of Children, 36*(4) 95-126. doi:10.1353/etc.2013.0037

Oberle, E., & Schonert-Reichl, K. A. (2016). Stress contagion in the classroom? The link between classroom teacher burnout and morning cortisol in elementary school students. *Social Science and Medicine, 159,* 30-37.

O'Brien, J. L., & Haaga, D. A. F. (2015). Empathic accuracy and compassion fatigue among therapist trainees. *Professional Psychology: Research and Practice, 46*(6), 414-420. http:// dx.doi.org/10.1037/pro0000037

Pardess, E., Mikulincer, M., Dekel, R., & Shaver, P. R. (2013). Dispositional attachment orientations, contextual variations in attachment security and compassion fatigue among volunteers working with traumatized individuals. *Journal of Personality, 82*(5), 355-366. doi: 10.1111/jopy12060

Pfifferling, J., & Gilley, K. (2000, April). Family practice management. Retrieved from http://www.aafg.org/fpm/2000/0400/p39.html

Pickering, C. (n.d.). The stress of work or the work of stress? *Canadian Teachers' Federation,* 15-20. Retrieved from http://www.ctf.fce.ca/Research- Library/Issue4_Article5_EN.pdf

Posen, D. (2013). *Is work killing you? A doctor's prescription for treating workplace stress.* Toronto, ON: Harper Collins.

Randler, C., Luffer, M., & Müller, M. (2015). Morningness in teachers is related to a higher sense of coherence and lower burnout. *Social Indicators Research, 122*(2), 595-606. doi: 10.1007/s11205-014-0699-2

Roeser, R. W., Schonert-Reichl, K. A., Jha, A., Cullen, M., Wallace, L., Wilensky, R., Harrison, J. (2013). Mindfulness training and reductions in teacher stress and burnout: Results from two randomized, waitlist-control field trials. *Journal of Educational Psychology, 105*(3), 787-804. doi:10.1037/a0032093

Russell, D. W., Altmaier, E., & Van Velzen, D. (1987). Job-related stress, social support, and burnout among classroom teachers. *Journal of Applied Psychology, 72*(2), 269-274.

Russell, M., & Brickell, M. (2015). The "double-edge sword" of human empathy: A unifying neurobehavioral theory of compassion stress injury. *Social Sciences, 4*(4), 1087-1117. doi:10.3390/socsci4041087

Schwarzer, R. & Hallum, S. (2008). Perceived teacher self-efficacy as a predictor of job stress and burnout: Mediation analyses. *Applied Psychology, 57*(s1), 152-171. doi:10.111/j.1464-0597.2008.00359.x

Schwarzer, R. & Jerusalem, M. (1995). Generalized self-efficacy scale. In J. Weinman, S. Wright & M. Johnston (Eds.). *Measures in health psychology: A user's portfolio, causal and control beliefs* (pp. 35-37). Windsor, UK: NFER-NELSON.

Skaalvik, E. M., & Skaalvik, S. (2016). Teacher stress and teacher self-efficacy as predictors of engagement, emotional exhaustion, and motivation to leave the teaching profession. *Creative Education, 7*(13), 1785-1799. http://dx.doi.org/10.4236/ce.2016.713182

Skinner, E., & Beers, J. (2016). Mindfulness and teachers' coping in the classroom: A developmental model of teacher stress, coping, and everyday resilience. In K. A. Schonert-Reichel & R. W. Roeser (Eds.), *Mindfulness in behavioral health handbook of mindfulness in education*: (pp. 99-118) New York, NY. Springer.

Soukhanov, A. H. (1984). *Webster's II new riverside university dictionary.* Boston, MA: Houghton-Mifflin.

Sprang, G., Clark, J. J., & Whitt-Woosley, A. (2007). Compassion fatigue, compassion satisfaction, and burnout: Factors impacting a professional's quality of life. *Journal of Loss and Trauma, 12*(3), 259-80. doi:10.1080/15325020701238093

Statistics Canada (2005). *Work Absence rates* (Catalogue no. 71-211). Retrieved from www.statscan.ca

Strong, E. K., Donnay, D. A. C., Morris, M. L., Schaubhut, N. A., & Thompson, R. C. (2008). Test review. *Rehabilitation Counselling Bulletin, 51*(2), 122-126.

Tuel, B., & Betz, N. E. (1998). Relationship of career self-efficacy expectations to the Myers-Briggs Type Indicator and personal styles scales. *Measurement and evaluation in counselling and development, 31*(3), 150-163.

Van Saane, N., Sluiter, J. K., Verbeek, J. H. A. M., & Frings-Dresen, M. H. W. (2003). Reliability and validity of instruments measuring job satisfaction–A systematic review. *Occupational Medicine, 53*(3), 191-200. doi:10.1095/occmed/kgq038.

Weiss, R. (1974). The provision of social relationships. In Z. Rubin (Ed.), *Doing unto others.* pp. 17-26. Englewood Cliffs, NJ: Prentice Hall.

Williams, S., & Cooper, C. L, (1998). Measuring occupational stress: Development of the Pressure Management Indicator. *Journal of Occupational Health Psychology, 3*(4), 306-321.

Zeidner, M., Hadar, D., Matthews, G., & Roberts, R. D. (2013). Personal factors related to compassion fatigue in health professionals. *Anxiety, Stress and Coping 26*(6), 595-609. doi:10.1080/10615806.2013.77045

ABOUT THE AUTHOR

I am a retired educator of 30 years. I have been involved with numerous changes in the education system. Throughout those years, I have seen changes in class size and dynamics; to curriculum re-writes and assessment practices. I have seen changes in administration at all levels and witnessed how they have impacted the system. I began to experience Compassion Fatigue (CF) or Occupational Stress Injury (OSI), but did not fully realize it until "something snapped". I feel that there is a need for discussion in the market regarding CF/OSI, specifically when training teachers for what can or could happen to them. And, for those in the system, to understand that there are ways to cope and survive.

Daryl lives in a rural southwestern Alberta community, where the foothills met the prairies, with his spouse of 30 plus years, JoAnna. They have three grown adult children. They are entertained by two cats, Nalli and Kalli, and their dog Max. Throughout the years, they have brought the world to them by hosting more than 20 foreign exchange students, who attended the local high school. He is a life-long learner, having just completed his second Master's program. He began his educational journey in Souris, MB attending the Souris Collegiate High School. After a short stint in the oil patch, he began his scholarly training at Brandon University (BU) in Brandon Manitoba, earning a Bachelor of Arts with a major in history and minors in political science and geography. At BU he met JoAnna. They moved to Calgary, Alberta, where after a time in retail, he took the initiative, to obtain his Bachelor of Education degree from the University of Calgary, becoming an elementary generalist. After graduation, he taught as a substitute with the Calgary Board of Education, and Foothills School Division until he landed a full-time teaching assignment with the Willow Creek School Division, now known as Livingstone Range School Division (LRSD). His love of learning was re-ignited seven years later when he enrolled in a Master of Arts in Educational Leadership through San Diego State University. He continued teaching with LRSD at various postings within the division. He successfully completed his second Masters of Counseling degree with City University of Seattle, with four years left until his 85-factor. He now spends his time building his clinical practice in Claresholm and Calgary, Alberta. He specializes in stress, anxiety, depression, and trauma.

CPSIA information can be obtained
at www.ICGtesting.com
Printed in the USA
LVHW110237060919
630098LV00001B/1/P